Breaking the Cycle of Women's Paid Domestic Work in Brazil

Breaking the Cycle of Women's Paid Domestic Work in Brazil:

A Study of Mothers and Daughters

By

Anna Maria Del Fiorentino

Cambridge
Scholars
Publishing

Breaking the Cycle of Women's Paid Domestic Work in Brazil:
A Study of Mothers and Daughters

By Anna Maria Del Fiorentino

This book first published 2023

Cambridge Scholars Publishing

Lady Stephenson Library, Newcastle upon Tyne, NE6 2PA, UK

British Library Cataloguing in Publication Data
A catalogue record for this book is available from the British Library

Copyright © 2023 by Anna Maria Del Fiorentino

All rights for this book reserved. No part of this book may be reproduced, stored in a retrieval system, or transmitted, in any form or by any means, electronic, mechanical, photocopying, recording or otherwise, without the prior permission of the copyright owner.

ISBN (10): 1-5275-0200-7
ISBN (13): 978-1-5275-0200-0

To all mothers fighting for a better future for their children, particularly those victims of an unequal society that takes so much from them and from their children.

Whatever we inherit from the fortunate
We have taken from the defeated

—T. S. Eliot, *Little Gidding*, Four Quartets

Table of Contents

Acknowledgements ix

Preface from the Brazilian Edition xiii

Preface to the English Edition xvi

Introduction xx

Literature Review and Methods... xxvi

Chapter One... 1
A Silent Strength (The Mothers)
   1.1 Marilla 3
   1.2 Dandara 4
   1.3 Val 9
   1.4 Vitória 14
   1.5 Carmem 18
   1.6 Findings 21

Chapter Two.. 25
A Job to Read and Write (The Daughters)
   2.1 Lucia 29
   2.2 Tereza.. 32
   2.3 Paula 35
   2.4 Helena 36
   2.5 Julia 39
   2.6 Findings 40

Chapter Three.. 43
Intertwined Memories (Mothers and Daughters)
   3.1 Marilla and Lucia.. 44
   3.2 Dandara and Tereza 48
   3.3 Val and Paula 61
   3.4 Vitória and Helena 62
   3.5 Carmem and Julia 64
   3.6 Findings 65

Chapter Four 67
Knowledge and Love (Conclusion)

References 71

ACKNOWLEDGEMENTS

The publication of this book is a project of many heads – and hearts – working together. I am very grateful for the incredible support I received along this new and sometimes challenging process of publishing my first book in English and in the UK. I give my thanks to Cambridge Scholars Publishing for accepting my manuscript and for guiding me through this world so professionally.

This book would not have been possible without the generosity of all the mothers and daughters from Brazil who dedicated their time to respond to my messages and shared their life stories. You are an inspiration – thank you.

I give my thanks to the Centre of Latin American Studies (CLAS) of the University of Cambridge for the support given during my master's studies, notably during the 2020–2021 global pandemic. I also extend a thank you to my CLAS master's colleagues for exchanging ideas and experiences with me, and to CLAS PhD candidate Beatriz Santos Barreto for valuable contributions to my research, and for friendship too. Also, I give my thanks to Sarah Abel, Grace Livingstone and Maite Conde for supervising my master's papers and teaching me so generously. I extend a thank you to Julie Coimbra and Chrisella de Vries for administrative support and for always being so friendly.

I give my thanks to the Faculty of Education at the University of Cambridge for offering me a place in their PhD programme – which I had just started before publishing this book. A special thanks must be given to Haira Gandolfi and my PhD supervisor Kathryn Moeller for receiving me with open arms at the Faculty of Education, guiding me through this new world – I couldn't be in better hands! I give my thanks to CLAREC (Cambridge Latin American Research in Education Collective) for being so friendly and accepting me as a member of this beautiful community.

A very special thank you goes to Murray Edwards College (Cambridge has a particular system where you are part of a faculty and a college). My college has been a place of women's empowerment and inspiration since the very beginning of my studies – and for many others before me, I am certain. I am very fortunate to have received the Vice-Chancellor's & Murray Edwards Scholarship via the Cambridge Trust for my PhD which is helping me to have "a room of my own" in this academic world. I am very grateful for meeting very supportive and inspirational people at Murray Edwards such as my college tutor Rachel Polonsky, Alex Piotrowski and current president Dorothy Byrne.

A special thanks to Ken Loach, whom I had the chance to meet in Cambridge at the screening of his movie "Sorry We Missed You" in 2023. His movies are highly inspirational to me; Chapter Two of this book "A Job to Read and Write" is named after a scene of the movie "Kes". Loach as a person is as inspirational as his work. He has an immense respect for people, honestly concerned with the struggles of the working class of this country, concerned with their concerns. I will always cherish the note of encouragement Loach sent me after we met (a reply to mine) and go back to it every time I feel powerless in my struggles: "we will all keep doing what we can, won't we!".

I give my thanks to Ms Gill Pavey for the incredible help proofreading my work in English. Without you this book would never have happened. Also, to my dear friend Marina Monzillo for helping me with the Brazilian Portuguese edition of this book, and with the quotes in Portuguese you will see in this English edition.

I extend my gratitude to my undergraduate professor Otaviano Canuto and Antônio Bizzo, my manager from when I worked at Banco do Brasil, at the London branch, for generously writing the recommendation letters sent for my master's application. And also to those who generously wrote recommendation letters for my PhD application; that is, Grace Livingstone and Pedro Mendes Loureiro.

I give my thanks to Christiano Tambascia and Rosana Pinheiro Machado for the guidance they gave me on my first steps to pursuing academic endeavours in the UK. A special thanks goes to Marcus Baccega for his faith in my return to academia and research work, non-stop encouragement and mentorship.

A special thanks goes to my master's dissertation supervisor, Pedro Mendes Loureiro, for inviting me to his discussion groups, for the critical support during my master's and for bringing in different perspectives that contributed to my research and beyond. Pedro has also generously contributed to this book by writing its Preface. Thank you, Pedro! When I grow up, I want to be just like you.

A warm thank you goes to Alexandre Trindade. We share the passion for transformations (within the University of Cambridge and beyond) and it has been a delight to join forces with you. Thank you for being the first to invite me to talk about my research work at the CLAREC *Whereabouts Seminar Series* in 2022. You are a good friend and an inspiration.

I would like to say thank you to my professors and undergraduate friends from the *Instituto de Economia* at *Universidade Estadual de Campinas* (UNICAMP) for the important role they have played in my formation as a whole and in the way I see the world.

A warm thank you goes to the teachers at my primary school, *Escola Comunitária de Campinas* (ECC), for awakening the love of learning in me, for giving me a progressive perspective on things and for instigating my critical thinking. And a general thank you goes to all the people that provided me with education – formal or informal, as education goes well beyond school borders. I believe that education is one of the most liberating experiences in our lives.

I give my thanks to the Anna Freud Centre for organizing events, many free of charge, about very important topics such as mental health in early years, the mother figure, the refugee crisis and the feeling of belonging, among many others. I got to know many interesting thinkers of our time, from outside my bubble, through events organized by the centre. I extend a thanks to Liz Pemberton from the Black Nursery Manager, a remarkable anti-racist specialist in early years education that I met in one of the centre's events – you will see some of her ideas in this book.

I extend a thank you to my friends outside of the academic world, for keeping me sane during this pandemic and always, notably Lilian Oliveira, Beatriz Lafraia, Cristina Scheeffer and Vanessa Pfeiffer. A special thanks goes to Felipe Catharino and Beatriz Lafraia for being the first to purchase a copy of my book when it was published in Brazil.

I give my thanks to Cleidia. You are my *muse of fire* for this work! And to all the invisibilized people that were or are a part of my life. Your life stories are not on most book pages but when they are told, they have this fundamental role of reclaiming humanity on those who are listening to them.

I give thanks to my parents, Anna and Luiz, and to my aunt Tetê for their unreserved love, the life values you taught me and for the immense support along the (long) way. The seeking of justice, the strength for the fight, the honest conversations and love, and the encouragement to question the world as it is – these are just a few examples among many others that were gifted to me by you since early childhood and always. I am also grateful for the newly published books you sent from Brazil that were incredibly valuable for my research. Also, I extend my thanks to my father-in-law Carlos Lungarzo for the enjoyable discussions about politics and human rights, for his valuable advice along the publication of my book. Thanks also to his wife Silvana, an inspiring mother and activist.

An important thank you goes to my husband Gui for the invaluable companionship and love. I am also very grateful for your help with the design of the cover of the Brazilian edition of my book and its internal content, making it to look just as I envisaged it.

Finally, I wish to say thank you to my children Thomas and Marco, for being an inspiration and my companions, discovering new passions and fights together – for encouraging me to keep fighting for a more fair, empathic and green world for when they grow older.

In memoriam Deborah Huggett

Preface from the Brazilian Edition

I will start this Preface with a warning if you like, warning the reader of a conflict of interests. I am wary about making an introduction to this work, which started as a master's dissertation and has now turned into a book. As the supervisor of this project and as someone who believes in its relevance, it is my duty to highlight its qualities. But I write light-hearted during this analysis. *Intertwined Memories*[1] addresses a highly important theme: the social mobility of the daughters of paid domestic workers in contemporary Brazil, from an angle that is strongly ignored – the role of family dynamics between mothers and daughters. By giving voice and agency to the protagonists of this process, the book portrays both with subtlety and with strength the stories of trauma, overcoming and healing that together, led to a fragile but undeniable experience of social mobility.

I will write this Preface without more ado, as the book speaks by itself and it is fair that I allow the reader to enjoy reading it at once. I will highlight, however, what are to me the major contributions and implications of the book. In my view, its essence is to give voice to the women that are the drivers of the process investigated by the research. Anna Maria is able to bring our attention to the personal and family efforts that, in all cases she analysed, were fundamental to cement upward social trajectories. It is not an overstatement to say that the reader will reach the end of the book feeling empathy for the women interviewed, after acquiring a glimpse of knowledge about the struggles experienced by the daughters to finish higher education and start their careers.

Equally important, and without denying the agency of the interviewees, Anna Maria does not make the mistake to assume that individual effort is sufficient strategy to reduce the inequalities that mark the Brazilian society. On the contrary, this is an assumption that runs through the book, even if it is not its centre. This way, the book brings forward the undeniable merits of

---

[1] The translation of the title of the Brazilian edition is *Intertwined Memories: Transforming Trauma into Empowerment* (in Portuguese: *Memórias Entrelaçadas: do Trauma ao Empoderamento*).

these successful life trajectories, which can be read in the light of the economic and institutional scenario that, as fragile as it was, limited the cases of success to the cases that required extraordinary agency from the daughters and their mothers.

The third greatest contribution of the book, although highly associated with the other two, is to highlight the role of the mothers in the process of their daughter's social mobility – and, coming from that, exploring how the trajectories and memories intertwine. There is vast literature about inequality in Brazil and Latin America, highlighting its variations, the social politics in relation to them, and the economics and social dynamics involved in this process. What Anna Maria's work brings to this debate, and this is done with particular sensibility, is to show how family trajectories are key elements to understand the experiences of upward social mobility and its limitations. By giving voice to the mothers, to their daughters, and inviting them to speak about each other the book shows the intricate arrangements that were established to help these women overcome trauma towards new careers and new lives.

Finally, the book also brings light to the extent of the experience of social mobility – once it is achieved. Precisely by telling the intertwined stories of mothers and daughters, Anna Maria shows that to start and to complete a higher education course goes well beyond a personal fulfilment or even a strictly professional one. As Dandara – a fictitious name of one of the mothers interviewed – says to her daughter when she was accepted into a master's programme at the University of São Paulo: "Daughter, you did it! WE did it!". To me, I can't see a more convincing demonstration of the urgent need of an effective social mobility agenda for Brazil as its results, as Anna Maria shows us though her interviewees, has the potential to cure and to result in gains that extend along generations.

I end this Preface with a reflection. *Mothers and Daughters* shows both the transforming power of social mobility and the deep difficulties encountered by the daughters of paid domestic workers in this process towards upward social mobility. The book also brings forward that such ascendant trajectories often do not pass through institutions and public policies, not uncommonly involving individual and family efforts to afford the fees of private universities – although the trajectories with higher social mobility were constructed, at least partially, with public (free) universities.

Writing this Preface in mid-2021, when a social mobility agenda seems like a distant memory in the current scenario of increasing inequality and oppression, my view is that the country should not attempt to reclaim former policies, although they are attractive if compared to present times. In my view, we need to pursue an effective and wider agenda for social inclusion that guarantee rights, dignity and autonomy instead of recreating fragile and oppressive experiences that, as Anna Maria shows, cannot be overcome without extraordinary combined efforts.

Enjoy your reading!

—Pedro Mendes Loureiro
Centre of Latin American Studies and Department of Politics and International Studies (CLAS-POLIS), Fitzwilliam College, University of Cambridge

Preface to the English Edition

I am a Brazilian woman who moved to London a little more than a decade ago. My children were born in London, and I have been a full-time mother since they arrived. Before that, I had a corporate career.

When our family decided to move from London to quiet Cambridge in 2018 at the time my youngest was about to start primary school, I timidly worked on a research project proposal to submit to the University of Cambridge. My aim was to pursue a master's degree that would help me to refresh myself after all those years being a full-time mum and, eventually, rejoin the job market afterwards. Little did I know that this experience would be more than a career change; it was the starting point of a new life in my forties. Age was against me in many ways as a mature student with parental responsibilities, but it was also on my side as, after a broad range of professional and life experiences, I was determined to pursue something meaningful, something that I believed would help, even if only a little, to create a better world, rather than bringing me immediate gains or an addition to my curriculum.

In the times of Trump, Brexit and the removal of President Dilma Rousseff in Brazil, I was driven by a high sense of opposition against the political forces that were gaining space in my home country and, indeed, all over the world. I wanted to show my children that there are many different ways of fighting those forces. I have to say, my children are my primary source of hope and inspiration for my academic work and most everything else.

It had been almost twenty years since I left university in Brazil, and targeting a place at the University of Cambridge was ambitious. I went to the university open day when I was still living in London; I spoke to people working in different departments and colleges. After that, I started working on a research proposal draft. I remember struggling to write an academic proposal in English, despite my experience with the language – writing academic material was like learning a new language to me. I showed my first draft to my husband and a few academic friends; I received their encouragement and, to cut a long story short, I was offered a place on the master's programme. Transitioning from being a full-time mum to a scholar was a bit of a shock but I received support in many different ways. However, pragmatically, if it was not for the financial support I have received from my family, I would probably never have started my studies despite receiving an offer, as I was not awarded a scholarship for my master's.

After some time being a full-time mother, I had lost the financial autonomy that I had before becoming a mother. More than that, my life choice put me behind in many other ways, in the short and long run: from the depreciation of my "market value" as a professional in search of a job, to a significant interruption in my pension plan. On top of that was the ordinary sexism, ageism and other "isms" that a woman faces when competing for places in the world.

Only after finishing my master's and publishing my first book in Brazil (based on my master's dissertation), did I start to see a little clearer what was the real force behind my research interests. It was my own experience of motherhood from the time I was a full-time mother, and the contrast of that period with other life moments, mainly to when I had a successful corporate career. When I was a full-time mother, I noticed that despite working more than I have ever worked before, people around me would often ask if I did not get bored of having so much time in my hands as I did not have a job. Others, with a more positive approach, would suggest that I took the opportunity of being away from my career to pursue other personal projects such a post-graduation project, or finding a hobby during my "spare" time. I struggled to see where was that free time that people were mentioning because if I was not busy with my children, I was certainly busy with our house and the family's domestic affairs. That was when I realized – honestly, I only understood that many years later – that what I did, the full-time work I was busy with looking after two young children in this "motherhood project" I put myself in, was completely invisible to others.

While in academia, I learned that my invisible work is called social reproductive labour, a work of care, often provided by women. In my case as a full-time mother, I experienced an unpaid type of reproductive work. That sense of invisibility connected me with other mothers, strangers and close friends, and with their struggles our struggles – as we dedicate ourselves to different forms of care work, paid or unpaid, and all we had to give up for us to benefit our children and family. And how fundamental, however invisible, what we do is to everyone around us, making our children and family feel safe, cared for and happy: that was my reference point and the force behind my academic work. I wanted to show the value of this invisible work of care and love and the difference it makes to the lives of those who benefit from it. I wanted to compare and contrast those experiences to when women (or whoever is in charge of the work of care in a family) don't have the opportunity – or when they are escaping from it, for many reasons – to dedicate themselves to the work of care of their own children. Experiencing life as a mother of young children and their experiences in early childhood, I wanted to show how the presence or absence of parental care in early childhood would impact the mental health of a person later in life. Ultimately, I believe, if the worth of reproductive work is finally perceived, that would encourage more people interacting with children – parents and non-parents – to dedicate themselves more freely to it, and that would bring a positive impact on children's mental health and society at large.

This book is based on the research work I conducted for my dissertation during my master's programme in Latin American Studies at the University of Cambridge, submitted in 2021. I spoke to mothers and daughters in Brazil with the purpose of understanding the invisibilized role of the mothers in experiences of social mobility of their daughters. The daughters were the first generation within their families to go to university and their mothers were paid domestic workers. Since then, my study has been adapted and translated into Brazilian Portuguese; a paperback edition was published by *Imaginário Coletivo* publishing house in Brazil at the end of 2021. This book is essentially based on my original master's dissertation, however its content was largely extended, as I had the liberty to include more quotes from my interviews and bring in new elements connected to my research that were available after I finished my master's.

You will find many original quotes from the mothers and daughters I interviewed in this book. By highlighting the experiences of those affected through their life stories, I aimed to reclaim humanity amid so many soulless academic texts and bring inspiration that, hopefully, might turn into social transformation. As Terence[1] said, a long time ago: "I am a man, I consider nothing that is human alien to me "[2]. I hope my readers will relate to the stories of the women I interviewed, as I did. Anyone, as a human, I believe, can resonate on a base or higher level, with the happy and sad life stories of the mothers and daughters you will see in this book. Every time I listen to the audio recordings sent to me by these women, I see and feel something new, I think of something else that was not there when I listened to it previously. I want my reader to have a similar experience when reading these stories and eventually, come to new, different conclusions from mine that will enrich the debate.

I hope you will enjoy this book.

---

[2] Publius Terentius Afer, known in English as Terence, was a notorious Roman African playwright during the Roman Republic. His original quotation, in Latin, is *Homo sum, humani nihil a me alienum puto*.

INTRODUCTION

Preta Rara's book *Me, Domestic Worker*[3] (2019) was the starting point of this study. The book is a collection of domestic worker's memories collected from the internet campaign #MeDomesticWorker[4], mostly related to experiences of trauma and abuse at work, including the author's own story – and the stories of her mother and grandmother who were also paid domestic workers. Many of the memories are told by daughters and a few by granddaughters and sons of domestic workers who are the first-generation entrants in higher education. Despite the main cause for the reduction in the number of young women working as domestic workers being the recent government programs which broadened access to higher education (IPEA, 2019), it caught my attention that most of the stories in this book hardly mention these programmes. Daughters and sons of domestic workers almost unanimously give credit to their mothers' sacrifices and support as they were a key contribution to their educational achievements and, in many cases, also social mobility after obtaining a university degree. This led to my first research question: why do they see their mothers as a central figure in their own academic achievements? What is the mother's role in this pursuit of further education for the younger generation?

I also observed in Preta Rara's book that the recollection of memories of domestic workers is overwhelmingly narrated by a third person. Only a few are told by domestic workers themselves. The mother's voice is rarely heard in feminist and psychoanalytic discourse, and their daughters tend to speak for them (Hirsch, 2012). I could confirm it by reading this book: the majority of the stories are narratives of the daughters, granddaughters and sons of domestic workers about their mothers' and grandmothers' life stories, recollections of experiences they were told by them but did not experience themselves. Why are domestic workers' voices so faint in this

---

[3] Original title *Eu, Empregada Doméstica*.
[4] #EuEmpregadaDoméstica.

campaign about themselves, differently from other testimonial campaigns such as *#MeToo* in which the stories are overwhelmingly narrated in the first person? It may be argued that the reason for the little direct engagement of domestic workers in this campaign is that the younger generation is more familiar with being involved with politics using social media while their mothers were engaged in other forms of activism, occupying different political spaces with much less reach than the internet (Da Silva, 2018). However, that would only partially explain their silence, which has led me to investigate further about other sources silencing domestic workers.

Lastly, in Preta Rara's book, I found that more than half of the stories from the daughters and sons about their mothers' experiences were mixed with their own memories. The reason for that is because they often lived the experiences together with their mothers. Many accompanied them to work when they were children, witnessing the abuse their mothers went through and therefore sharing the trauma too. Many of the domestic workers' children experienced early separation from their mothers, and loss and trauma as a result of their mothers working long hours. Contexts of poverty and the informality of the occupation were responsible for mothers working extended hours, limiting their capacity of caregiving for their children, breaking up the important psychological ties that develop over time between a child and the mother, as their mothers were unable to provide for their day-to-day care (Goldstein et al., 1980a).

Brazil is the country with the highest number of domestic workers (ILO, 2018); they are the second largest occupational group of women in the country (Melleiro & Heuser, 2020) and represent 14,6% of women in the labour market; 92% are women and 63% are black (IPEA, 2019). They have the lowest wages and are subjected to constant discrimination, harassment, violence and abandonment (Almeida, 2019; IPEA, 2019), positioning domestic workers as one of the most vulnerable groups of workers (Fish, 2017). The occupation has been passed historically from mothers to daughters, a social reproduction of paid – and often also underpaid or unpaid – reproductive labour.

Duffy (2007) investigates the role of social reproductive labour on the gendered division of work and women's subordination from an historical perspective. Reproductive labour, a concept originally created by Marxist economics, was developed further in history to designate the invisible work produced by women's unpaid work in the home that was indispensable to the reproduction of the productive labour force. Such "women's work" includes domestic, cooking and caring work that are "necessary to maintain existing life and to reproduce the next generation" (p. 316). The concept was widened to embrace the spheres of paid reproductive work when women joined the paid labour force. Domestic work, paid and unpaid, remain unvalued in contrast to other occupations. Duffy also analyses the racialized hierarchy in reproductive labour through an intersectional lens and calls the tasks historically performed by non-white women the "dirty work" of reproductive labour (p. 317), highlighting the racial division among women carrying out reproductive work.

Because women are often in charge of most caregiving responsibilities at home and within their communities, they often end up participating less in the formal workforce. They often have to take a break in their careers or reduce the hours worked in paid jobs after having children. This disruption is felt in the short term, contributing to gender pay gaps for example, but also in the long run, eventually resulting in women's poverty and social exclusion in later life (European Commission, 2015). Childcare is currently unrecognized in most state pension systems, as the time spent by mothers looking after their own children, full-time when they are little, is unwaged (Ginn, 2001). The issue has begun to be addressed by policymakers, as Argentina created a new government programme in 2021 to recognize rights for women who worked as caregivers, wherein women could gain up to three years of social security contributions for each child they had (Alcoba, 2021). Still, we are far from addressing the gender gap in most state pension systems as mothers' unpaid caregiving to their children at home is still not perceived as an occupation.

Paid domestic work is also frequently not seen as work, invisibilized by policymakers and society in general. Only in 2013 did a constitutional reform, and its associated law in 2015, establish equal labour rights for domestic workers in Brazil, contributing to the professionalization of the occupation (Lima & Prates, 2019). However, despite this progress, the newly gained rights were not given to self-employed domestic workers working in several households (Acciari, 2018), and this occupation is still excluded from the Labour Code, lacking extension of all labour rights.

According to IPEA (2017), informality levels are high in paid domestic work: only 29.3% of black domestic workers and 32.5% of white were formally employed in 2015; the formalization is more present in prosperous areas of the country, while it is still sparse in poorer areas such as the northeast. The new legislation made it more expensive for families to employ domestic workers full-time, leading to an increase in self-employed domestic workers working in several households, not covered by labour rights. The same studies show that despite experiencing an increase in income from 1995-2015, domestic workers on average were paid less than the national minimum wage. Also, the occupation is in the course of ageing: while more than 50% of domestic workers were younger than twenty-nine years old from 1995 to 2005, only 16% of them were in this age group in 2015. This indicates that a large proportion of young women are escaping from domestic work – but what has enabled them to break the cycle of domestic work within their families?

Much has been written about the positive results of the expansion of the network of federal universities and affirmative action policies implemented in Brazil during the Workers' Party (PT) federal administrations (2003–2016) (Fonseca, 2018; Marques et al., 2018; Picanço, 2016; Moreira Damasceno & de Andrade, 2016, among others). However, there is very little written about the social mobility that was eventually promoted by it (Alves Cordeiro, 2013). Still, the role of the families on this journey towards social mobility of the younger generation remains unexplored. Also, there is a lack of gaze on women's mobility since class studies in Brazil have traditionally gathered data from the male head of family and their sons (Pastore, 1982; Pastore & Valle Silva, 2000). This ignores the substantial change in women's engagement with their families and the world as they joined the labour market in Brazil, and elsewhere (Goldthorpe et al., 1987).

I interviewed five pairs of mothers and daughters: four mothers are or were paid domestic workers, and one mother was a cleaner in a state-funded school. I included the school cleaner's stories to enrich my analysis, as the social relationship between school cleaners and other members of the school staff is very similar to the one of domestic workers and their employers. According to Machado Chaves (2000), when middle-class women in Brazil first entered the labour market, they tended to go into teaching jobs to complement their father's or husband's income. She argues that they became "housewives-teachers"[5] (p. 138), while cooking and cleaning jobs were occupied by women that "naturally" had these skills, notably poor, non-white and with low levels of education, extending the domestic environment into schools "[...] where the headteacher is the housewife and the school cleaning lady is there to please her. A personal relationship between domestic worker and her employer"[6] (p. 138).

All of the daughters I interviewed were part of the first generation in their families to go to university. Despite the sons of domestic workers also having benefited from the wider access to higher education, I focus on the daughters as I aim to understand further how they broke the cycle of domestic work historically passed from mothers to daughters in the country.

This book will explore the role of the families, particularly the mothers of the first-generation entrants into higher education during this process. I will investigate their daughters' eventual social mobility in terms of occupation as well as some sense of family income, gathered from the life stories of the women I interviewed. I argue that the families of the first-generation entrants in higher education, as much as the important governmental changes that helped the democratization of higher education in the country, have a key role in this process and are often overlooked. I argue that the sacrifices of these mothers were of high importance for their daughters to enter higher education. To make sense of these results, I introduce the concept of *intertwined memories* to explain how these women supported each other in this process that changed the social position of the younger generation and moreover, helped mothers and daughters to transform experiences of trauma and abuse into empowerment. I argue that the social mobility achieved by the daughters has lifted their mothers as well, not in terms of income or class necessarily but in terms of well-being, having better, more fulfilled lives.

After this introduction, the book is structured into a chapter dedicated to the literature review and methods, then three chapters based on my interviews, and the conclusion. In the first chapter, "A Silent Strength", I investigate the life stories of domestic workers and how acute poverty and the lack of formal education drove them into paid domestic work, along with

---

[5] "Mulheres-professoras".
[6] "(…) onde a diretora é a dona de casa e a servente vai fazer aquela gentileza. Uma relação pessoal de patroa e empregada".

the experiences of trauma that silenced their voices. The following chapter, "A Job to Read and Write", I explore the multiple factors that enabled the daughters of domestic workers to enter university, as well as whether they have experienced social mobility or not after obtaining a degree. The third chapter, "Intertwined Memories", is a combination of stories from both mothers and daughters. I explore how these women supported and empowered each other, and how the presence or absence of the mothers' care during early childhood impacted the lives of their now adult daughters. I will investigate further how an eventual social mobility from the daughters bounced back to their mothers, allowing them to experience better lives and repair trauma. Each main chapter is divided in six subsections, one for each woman I have interviewed as well as a final one with my findings. Highlighting each woman in the subchapters was the best way I found to give agency to each person I interviewed and their stories.

LITERATURE REVIEW AND METHODS

A society in which the success or failure of children with equal ability depends on the socio-economic status of their parents is not a fair one (McKnight, 2015). Unequal access to education reproduces inequalities as the probability of achieving significant social mobility through education is considerably smaller at each step down the class structure. This is because students from lower classes tend to leave school earlier compared to those from upper classes, and the chances of succeeding are smaller as they try to re-enter the system after dropping out (Labaree, 1997).

Different national campaigns and educational reforms were established in Brazil to help overcome illiteracy in the country (Xavier, 2019). EJA[7] (Education for Young and Adults) is one of these programmes – also popularly known among the women I interviewed by its former name, *Supletivo*. This programme is aimed at youths and adults who left school before finishing it, offering fast-track primary and secondary education in a shorter time and flexible hours. It provides a certificate of primary or secondary education once the student passes the national exams, giving them credentials to pursue further academic endeavours (e.g. higher education if secondary education has been completed) and serving as proof of qualification, often required in job applications. Most of the domestic workers I interviewed, and one of the daughters, caught up with primary or secondary education through these programmes, as you will see in later chapters.

As formal education has become more available over the years in Brazil, popular pressure to equalize access to it has continually widened. Widening access to post-secondary education has for a long time been a political issue (Billingham, 2018; McKnight, 2015), but only in the early 2000s was the education system changed more deeply in the country. This occurred during the *Pink Tide*, the political turn to the left in Latin American countries which in Brazil started with Lula's government in 2003 and lasted until the

---

[7] Educação para Jovens e Adultos.

impeachment of President Dilma in 2016 (Grigera, 2017). The Worker's Party administration introduced Reuni[8] (Programme to Support Restructuring Plans and the Expansion of Federal Universities), expanding the network of federal universities. New institutions were created as well as new campuses for existing ones, focusing on inland and remote areas of the country to serve rural and deprived areas (Bizerril, 2018). In addition, new funding programmes for higher education were created such as ProUni[9] (The University for All Programme) while the existing FIES[10] (Student Financing Fund) was expanded to support low-income students in private universities (Fonseca, 2018). This increased the number of students in private universities, a contentious issue as some argued that students with a privileged background were still "hoarding opportunities" (McKnight, 2015) and occupying the limited number of places available at public universities (Carvalho, 2013), while the commodification of higher education led disadvantaged students to seek low-quality education in the private sector (Marques et al., 2018). The government programmes therefore benefited a growing number of new, for-profit institutions (Carvalho, 2013).

Educational stratification is present at all levels in Brazil. State-funded schools provide education free of charge, while private schools are fee-paying and are perceived as the most exclusive and prestigious in the country. The best education available at primary and secondary levels is mostly offered privately and, quite often, is expensive. I will use the concept of "public" education here differently from how the term is used in England and Wales where a "public school" is a fee-charging institution, public in the sense of being open to all who can afford it. When I name a "public" school or university in Brazil I will refer to state-funded ones, as opposed to fee charging which will be referred to as "private".

While top schools that prepare students to enter elite universities are private and are unaffordable to the working class, top universities in Brazil are public and free of charge. They are funded either at federal or state level. Private universities charge tuition fees; some are costly while other, for-profit institutions offer cheaper, low-quality education. Because of this,

---

[8] Programa de Apoio a Planos de Reestruturação e Expansão das Universidades Federais.
[9] Programa Universidade para Todos.
[10] Fundo de Financiamento Estudantil.

securing a place at a public university is challenging and elitist, as places are often offered to students of higher social classes that are able to afford private schools and the preparatory courses to pass the notoriously difficult university admission tests. Similarly to what Labaree (1997) describes about the US context, the process of widening access to higher education in Brazil during the early 2000s promoted equality, but also adapted itself to the inequality and stratification that preceded it.

The criteria for entering higher education were also changed during this period. Affirmative actions such as the racial quota system were introduced at federal universities, helping to close the gap between white and non-white individuals (Ribeiro, 2018; Jensen, 2010). Based on the quota system, 50% of places in Brazil's federal universities were reserved either for students coming from government-funded schools or low-income families, who are of African or indigenous descent (Fonseca, 2018). The positive results were quickly visible as non-whites were, for the first time, a majority at federal universities in 2018 (IBGE, 2019). State universities followed, creating their own affirmative action programmes that are also leading to effective changes (Cosme, 2021).

Widening access to higher education in Brazil happened in a favourable context, accompanied by economic growth, low inflation, job creation and the increase in the real living wage, along with the introduction of cash transfer programmes and the Zero Hunger programme, among others. Together, they have changed the lives of many, contributing to a significant decrease in poverty and hunger, and driving the country towards greater income equality (United Nations, 2014). The combination of these new policies and the positive scenario that was created drove a great number of disadvantaged young people into university, the majority of which were the first generation within their families to go to university in Brazil – this new influx included the daughters of domestic workers. The country experienced what some called a "silent revolution" (Brito, 2018) and many young women broke out of the family cycle of paid domestic work as a result. However, this progress has been under threat by the economic downturn in mid-2014 and by the more recent installation of a conservative, male-dominated government (Gates Foundation, 2017). In addition to that, uneven recovery paths across and within countries since the 2020-2021 global pandemic are likely to affect young, low-skilled women more, especially in emerging markets and developing economies such as that in Brazil (Gopinath, 2021; Canuto & Zhang, 2021).

Higher education plays an important role in enabling upward social mobility, but a degree per se will not translate into social mobility as other conditions are required, whether on a macroeconomic level such as level of employment, at the university environment or at home. The latter is the object of this research.

In his book *On Education*, Russell (2009) distinguished "education of character" from "education in knowledge" (p. ix), the first being particularly important in the early years. He argued that neither character nor intelligence will develop as well or as freely if there is a deficiency of love given to the child during their first years of education, and that society can only be transformed if the basis of education is knowledge wielded by love. More than just acknowledging social mobility in a material sense, this book aimed to explore the education of character, reimagined here as the formation of the identities of the first-generation entrants in higher education. I will investigate how the experiences in early childhood affected their well-being and mental health in adulthood, a novel approach to exploring lifelong generational inequalities. For this reason, understanding the intergeneration transmission of these women's memories was a key element in my work.

Hirsch (2012) and the theory of postmemory was the starting point to explore the transmission of memory between domestic workers and their daughters. Her theory was created in the context of the Holocaust and the discussion of historical trauma, memory and forgetting. She argues that the memory of certain extreme experiences can be transferred from Holocaust survivors to their children, despite the younger ones not being present at the event (Hirsch, 2012). Sarlo (2005) has developed Hirsch's concept further, applying it to the context of the Argentinian dictatorship and the transmission of memories of persecution, torture and disappearance from a generation of parents that fought against the dictatorship, to their children. I build upon Hirsch's concept of postmemory by exploring the dynamics of memory transmission between mothers and daughters, in the context of acute poverty and multiple oppressions that led these mothers to experiences of trauma and abuse, often present in their daughters' memories and identities as well.

I noticed in my interviews that when gathering stories of trauma I often encountered silence as a response, and new approaches were therefore required. Traumatic memories were "forgotten", often omitted by the mothers, while their daughters, despite not always sharing their traumatic memories were keener to talk about their feelings.

Silence is frequently associated with remembrance rather than forgetting. Pollak (1993) explored the political silence in Germany after the WWII period and the ambivalence of feelings of the victims associated with traumatic memories, including guilt and embarrassment. He argues that silence is also personal rather than political and is often used to protect the younger generations from the scars of their parents. Also, he argues that silence is a way to cope when a person is a victim of a social classification that perceives them as invisible and inferior. He calls these forms of silenced memories, "underground memories"[11]. They are kept alive through informal ways of communication, transmitted within families or specific groups and, differently from the "official" collective memory, they are not generally available. Eventually, the weight of the silence is too heavy (Lorde, 1984) and these memories overflow, invading the public space and initiating public conversations. The unsaid, marginalized memories then – quite frequently – transform into protest and a demand for justice.

I have previously discussed social mobility for the domestic workers' daughters and argued that higher education is insufficient to explain this mobility, requiring further investigation about intrafamily relations by bringing up memories. For the latter, I have interviewed five pairs of mothers and daughters: Marilla and Lucia, Dandara and Tereza, Val and Paula, Vitória and Helena, and Carmem and Julia.

Mothers and daughters were selected according to the following criteria: i) mothers had to be or have been paid domestic workers, including cleaners and carers providing services within a private house. I widened these criteria and collected a few stories from school cleaners as well; ii) daughters had to be the first generation in their families to obtain a higher education degree, either an academic or a professional one; iv) daughters had to have started university during the early 2000s and had finished it. I was not actively looking for daughters that were benefited by the affirmative action

---

[11] *Mémoire souterraines* as opposed to the *mémoires officielle* (Pollak, 1993, p. 18).

policies and the expansion of the federal university network, and I was open to interviewing women that went to either public or private universities.

I interviewed a diverse range of women. The youngest mother was fifty-one years old and the oldest was seventy-four at the time of our first interviews. The youngest daughter was twenty-six, and the oldest daughter was forty-two. One pair of interviewees voluntarily declared themselves black, one daughter declared herself and her mother as of Japanese descent and the others did not share racial identity details as they were not asked. These women's narratives are presented in detail throughout the book.

I never met these women in person or knew them previously to our conversations, except for one pair of interviewees that are from my home town. Most names were suggested by people from my personal network. They introduced me to these women and the mothers have further introduced me to their daughters or vice versa. I spoke to participants separately.

Conversations happened in the extraordinary context of a global pandemic, in 2020-2021. I conducted semi-structured, in-depth interviews to gather these women's life stories. Interviews were held using an innovative method: most interviews were not in real time, face to face, but through recorded audio messages using the Whatsapp mobile platform. I sent two different sets of questions, one to the mothers and one to their daughters via a text message, and encouraged them to reply using recorded audio messages. I opted for this method firstly because communication via recorded audio messages on Whatsapp is a popular form of communication in Brazil, and was a good alternative form of communication during the Covid-19 pandemic, especially as I am in the UK and these women are in Brazil. Secondly, because some of these women have very restricted free time, with some domestic workers spending most of their time at their employers' house and some daughters I interviewed having babies at home – in this case, a recorded answer would allow them to identify the best time to reply, based on their availability and privacy. Thirdly, the process of recording the message proved to be a very efficient way to gain quick intimacy with the interviewees. I argue that it was more efficient than meeting these women in person as the exchange of recorded messages brought on an additional layer of intimacy. The process of recording those messages worked like keeping a shared journal, or presenting a monologue directed by the women themselves. The participants were replying to my questions, but they were not directly speaking to me, a stranger to them; they were speaking to themselves alone about their memories and experiences, at their chosen places and time. I have confirmed that by the answers received: the recorded ones were denser and more intimate compared to the few I have received in writing and the one conducted in real time, by telephone. Also, this process allowed a fair share of power during the interviews, as participants had more control during the process, recording their answers themselves, spontaneously sending additional information and, eventually, reconsidering the recorded content and deleting it before sending to me. This gave them more agency to communicate their boundaries better.

I received a few text messages as responses, and in only one case I had to call an interviewee on her landline in Brazil as she is not acquainted with smartphones, hence the reason I opted for a more traditional approach. The conversations were recorded with the person's agreement and the women's names were changed to keep their identity anonymous. I purposely avoided asking direct questions that could trigger strong emotional responses as they revived old, traumatic memories and I prepared a relaxed, informal environment to encourage them to go deeper into their memories but leaving the decision to share or not to share their stories to themselves. I was not a passive listener in my interviews; I shared with them my own life stories when they were relevant to our conversations. In most cases I recorded audio messages to reply to their responses, and in few cases I responded by text messages.

My focus since the beginning of this project was to give the floor to the women I interviewed, hence why the reader will find many passages in this book as they were spoken on the recorded audio messages I received. I tried to keep their informal style and vocabulary while translating the original quotes in Portuguese to English myself, keeping true to their original meaning, adapting words rather than literally translating them. I kept the original transcripts in Portuguese as footnotes for the more adventurous readers.

In between finishing my interviews and publishing this book, I stayed in contact with some of the women I interviewed. With some, I exchange quick messages on Mother's Day and Christmas. With some others, from time to time we speak about key life events, such as the start of my PhD or the divorce and death of the father of one of the participants.

To show my gratitude to my participants, I sent a copy of the Brazilian edition of my book to all the families I interviewed soon after it was published in 2021. I also met some of these women in person when I visited Brazil in 2022 and had the opportunity to show my gratitude in our face-to-face meetings.

CHAPTER ONE

A SILENT STRENGTH (THE MOTHERS)

What I couldn't have ... my children have now.[12] (Dandara)

Child and adolescent psychotherapist Sarah Peter defines trauma as a single, frightening incident that disrupts someone's feeling of safety in a very serious way (Anna Freud Centre, 2022). Trauma has different dimensions and distinctions. This book will explore three types of trauma: psychological; social; and vicarious or secondary trauma. Wise (2007) summarized these types of traumas in the book *Trauma Transformed*: psychological trauma refers to critical experiences that affect how people function, such as emotional abuse or neglect. Social trauma refers to social conditions that perpetuate forms of oppression against minoritized groups such as discrimination. Secondary trauma refers to the stress experienced by family, friends or professionals as a result of their empathy while caring for others that experienced traumatic events or ongoing trauma.

According to Peter (Anna Freud Centre, 2022), development trauma or childhood trauma is a mixture of chronic experiences in the earliest years of an infant, toddler or child when having their caregiving disrupted. That often includes abuse or neglect, but it can also be due to multiple separations and disruptions, and mental health difficulties in family members. She argues that it is important to highlight the social context of trauma since children who have experienced developmental trauma rarely experience it because the parent is failing them intentionally. She adds that trauma in the early years is almost invariably linked to the social context of the family such as experiences of poverty, failures of government, war, intergenerational cycles of poverty that are not being broken, systemic discrimination and racism. She argues that the consequences of these challenging contexts will have an impact on children and their families' mental health. It will also

---

[12] "O que eu não pude ter, os meus tem".

affect the relationships between parents and children as well as the capacity of parents and families to provide good parenting to their children, having significant and long-term consequences on their lives.

An in-depth understanding of the contexts surrounding the lives of the women I interviewed was fundamental for my analysis, and to point out the humanity behind each life story. Some mothers showed feelings of guilt during our conversations, believing they had failed their children when their best was not enough – most often due to highly unfavourable contexts. Likewise, some of the daughters showed resentment toward their mothers as they feel they were abandoned and neglected by them during their childhoods. In most cases, now they are adult women themselves, the daughters showed that they are able to understand that the socio-economic context of their parents did not allow them to do better. However, despite understanding that, they mourn for a time that was lost, the lost opportunity of having their mothers around when they were little.

The domestic workers I interviewed experienced traumatic experiences during their lifetime. I learned about them in our conversations, partially from themselves and partially from their daughters' narratives. Experiences of trauma and workplace indignity were the driving force leading these mothers to prioritize their daughter's education – often at the cost of their own ambitions. They strongly objected to their daughters becoming paid domestic workers, being subjected to the same conditions they were and often, also what their mothers and grandmothers experienced. They wanted their daughters to have a more formal education than they had, and they all had high hopes that a degree would translate into a dignified job and life. When I use the word "dignified" I mean dignity as a fundamental human right, the worth of a human person (United Nations, 2015) as opposed to the indignity often experienced when these women are exploited, abused, silenced and invisibilized.

All the mothers and daughters I interviewed have a good relationship, and the daughters show gratitude for their mother's efforts in their narratives. However, the happy memories of life achievements of the younger generation are often accompanied by resentment related to the share of their mother's traumas. Although the daughters did not experience the same level of deprivation that their mothers did, they carry this "genetic trauma" from them. This chapter will explore the life stories of the domestic workers; some are richer in details while others are more restricted, based on the information I gathered from my interviews. It will present an overview of the mother's traumatic experiences as well as investigating their role in supporting their daughters' pursuit of higher education.

1.1 Marilla

Marilla's parents were Japanese immigrants. She was born and raised in her parent's small rural property in Sorocaba (São Paulo). The family was very poor, and she and her siblings worked on the family's land from when they were children until she moved away to a bigger city to become a domestic worker. Later, she was offered a job as school cleaner and worked at this position for twenty-five years. She avoided talking about her problems: "I believe I have the perfect life"[13], she told me in our conversation. However, I have learned from my interview with her younger daughter, Lucia, that her mother was marked by traumatic experiences such as losing all of her teeth when still young due to the lack of means to afford dental care. As the youngest child, Lucia told me that she witnessed the worst moments of her mother's life. She told me that by the time she was born, her mother had lost her hopes and was full of resentment because of her traumatic life experiences. She recalls:

> *One of my siblings was born with an intellectual disability; I am the youngest one, right, so, it was like, a very difficult life. The stories she [Marilla] told [the children] about her search for cheaper milk [to give to the children] ... My mother tells, right, that she used to have, like, nice qualities, but life turned her into a rough person, you know. So, when I came in, I encountered a very rough mother, a person, like, depressed, very resentful*[14]. (Lucia)

---

[13] "Minha vida eu acho ótima".
[14] "Um dos meus irmãos inclusive nasceu com atraso mental; eu sou a caçula, né, então, foi assim, uma vida muito difícil. Essa coisa que ela contava, de buscar o leite C [mais barato, para dar para as crianças] ... Minha mãe, ela conta, né, que até ela era, assim, um pouco prendada, mas a vida foi fazendo ela ficar uma pessoa dura, sabe. Então eu já cresci com a minha mãe muito dura, uma pessoa, assim, deprimida, muito amargurada."

Marilla has five children; one was born with an intellectual disability. She struggled to work and provide additional care for her child with special needs: "it was a very difficult time and perhaps I have abandoned them [her children] a little"[15], she says, showing guilt for not having enough time to look after her other children. Despite that, she caught up with her secondary school studies when she was forty-five years old. Then, she passed a test to be a cleaner in a Court of Justice in São Paulo – that required complete secondary education – where she worked for the last ten years before retiring. Her last job gave her stability and a higher income, allowing her to pay for English lessons for Lucia as well as paying for a one-year preparation course to help her daughter pass the university admission test. When Lucia went to university and left her parents' home, Marilla told me that she still helped her: "I brought her home-made food every week, I washed her clothes, brought stuff in and out … you know … those things that only a mother would do"[16], she says.

When asked about life opportunities she wished her daughter had she said: "I wish that she studied law ..."[17] (Lucia studied languages and literature, not law), "... there is still time! She can easily do it before she is sixty!"[18], she added.

1.2 Dandara

Dandara started working in a factory when she was thirteen years old to help her parents and her eleven siblings. "I had no opportunities in life"[19], she says. When talking about her life's lack of opportunities, she recalls that her mother's dream was that she would become a seamstress – a good occupation for women at her time. She says:

> I didn't have, let's say, this opportunity [of studying, like her daughter had] because my parents, right ... they ... they needed a lot [of financial help], right. So, the dream, like, my mother's [dream] – look what my mother saw

---

[15] "Foi uma época muito difícil e talvez eu tenha abandonado um pouco eles".
[16] "Eu levava comida pronta pra ela toda semana, lavava a roupa dela, trazia e levava ... essas coisas assim, de uma mãe, né?"
[17] "Eu gostaria que ela fizesse Direito".
[18] "Ainda tem tempo! Até sessenta anos dá bem pra fazer".
[19] "Oportunidades não tive".

as an opportunity for me – was that I was a seamstress, understand, right. In the old days it was to be a seamstress; I never liked it, like, [never liked] sewing. What I did like was to fight and there I went, with thirteen and a half years, I started working in a factory and, there, I keep on working as a weaver, right. And weavers earned, like, quite a good sum, understand. So, I did help my parents very, very much indeed. So, I only went to factories, from 6 am to 2 pm, in the following week from 2 pm to 10 pm. So, I didn't have that space [to study], right. I didn't have ... that opportunity, like, to study[20]. (Dandara)

Dandara told me that her mother had even fewer opportunities than herself as she was married about the age of eleven and her mother's grandmother was an enslaved person:

My mother too, she too [did not have opportunities in life] ... My mother married ... she was twelve when she married]? My mum became a mother when she was fifteen years of age, right. So, she didn't have opportunities, what she had was, like ... was that thing, right, of being a housewife, raise the children.[21] (Dandara)

Dandara told me more about her mother having to escape from where she was, but did not give me more details about the reasons behind her escape:

My mother came from the countryside, Passos, Minas Gerais. My mother was a widow when she was very young because when my mother got married ... I think she was eleven, she didn't even have her [first] period. When my

---

[20] "Eu não tive muito assim essa oportunidade [de estudar] porque meus pais, né ... já ... precisava bastante, né. Então, o sonho, assim, da minha mãe – olha a oportunidade de minha mãe - era de eu sê costureira, entendeu, né. Antigamente era mais costura; e eu nunca gostei, assim, de costura: eu gostava de ir pra luta e eu fui com meus treze anos e meio, eu entrei numa fábrica, e ali eu fui trabalhando, a tecelã, né. E a tecelã ganhava, assim, razoavelmente, entendeu. Então, eu ajudava muito, muito meus pais. Então eu entrava só em firma em fábrica, das 6 às 2, outra semana das 2 às 10. Então eu não tive aquele espaço [pra estudar], né. Não tive... aquela oportunidade assim, de estudá".

[21] "Minha mãe também, ela também ... Minha mãe casou minha mãe tinha doze anos? Minha mãe foi mãe com quinze anos de idade, né. Então não teve oportunidade que ela teve coisa assim ... é aquela coisa, né, de sê dona de casa, criar os filhos."

mother had her first period, she was about fifteen years old, that's when she got pregnant, right. And my mother had to escape, she came in a truck with her children, she escaped, understand[22]. (Dandara)

Dandara worked mainly as a cleaner in a state-funded school in São Paulo, for many years. She is now retired but still works at her family's food stall selling African food. She caught up with primary education when she was an adult.

She described the work she used to do when working at the school and compares it to what her daughter is doing now:

I was a school cleaner, I worked in a school, right. [I] worked at school, [I] did laundry, cook, I cleaned the bathrooms, right. I also looked after the children, right. I always say: it's not that ... I am proud of the work I did being a washer woman, ironing ... thanks to God, my daughter is now a doctor! [Dandara laughs an enjoyable laugh] Right? So ... these things ... this pride that I felt, right ... this pride that I feel! And there are still many things ahead. There are many things ahead because – thanks to God, right – she [Tereza] is doing her doctorate, right[23]. (Dandara)

Dandara told me that she lives in a poor community in São Paulo and that she was concerned to have her children raised "on the streets", so she and her husband were constantly looking for learning opportunities to keep them busy:

[We] really looked out for support, for courses [for their children], right. Saying: look, they've opened a course, let's do it, right. Because I didn't like

---

[22] "A minha mãe, ela veio do interior, Passos, Minas Gerais. Minha mãe ficô viúva muito nova porque minha mãe casô ... acho que [com] onze ano, minha mãe não tinha nem menstruação. Quando minha mãe foi menstruar, minha mãe tinha quinze ano, foi aonde que ela ficô grávida do meu irmão mais velho, né. E minha mãe, ela veio fugida, com os filhos dela, veio num caminhão, fugida, entendeu."

[23] "Eu fui servente, trabalhei numa escola, né. Trabalho na escola, lavadeira ... cozinheira, lavadeira de banheiro, né. Cuidava também das crianças, né. E eu sempre falei assim: não é que ... eu tenho orgulho do que eu fiz sendo lavadeira, passadeira ... Graças a deus, hoje a minha filha é doutora! [Dandara ri uma risada gostosa] Né?. Então ... essas coisas ... esse orgulho que eu tive, né ... que eu tenho! E tem muitas coisa ainda pra frente. Tem muitas coisa pra frente porque – graças a deus, né – ela tá fazendo doutorado, né".

to see my children on the streets, so, all the courses available ... like ... every single one, when it was good for them, we went for it, okay? We helped a lot in this sense, we really helped. I also had, thank God, many helps, right, like, the help from the people [of her community] that saw, right, the struggles, our struggles, like, they said, look, Dandara, João [husband], there is a course there! ... and there I went, enrolling Tereza and Gabriel [her other child] on it, understand. We gave them this support [saying] you have to study![24] (Dandara)

I interviewed her older daughter, Tereza. Both mother and daughter spontaneously declared themselves black women.

The lives of black people living in the most deprived areas of São Paulo like Dandara and her family are constantly subjugated to the power of death (Amparo Alvis, 2018), victims of the necropolitics (Mbembe, 2003). According to Adão (2018, Abstract), "There is a perverse link between vulnerability to death and race in the urban space of São Paulo city [...]" making Dandara and her family highly vulnerable because of their race, on top of other oppressions they face. Dandara is particularly concerned about structural racism in Brazil and its implications on her children's lives. Since their early years, she constantly told them *"you can achieve anything a white person can achieve"*[25] and taught them to be proud of their African ancestry.

Dandara and her husband did not want their children to work before finishing secondary education and gave them the opportunity to focus on their studies. She says: "this opportunity [to study] I gave them, right, to my children. I didn't want her [Tereza] to go through, like, through what I went through"[26]. The parents nurtured an intellectual environment at home: "the most important space for learning is at home ... it is within ourselves, within

---

[24] "Ia muito atrás mesmo de apoio, de curso, né. Fala: óia, abriu um curso, vâmo fazê!", né. Porque eu não gostava de criar meu flho na rua, então, todos o curso que tivesse ... assim ... na VIDA, que era bom pra eles, a gente ia em frente, tá? A gente ajudou nessa parte, ajudou mesmo. E eu tive também, graças a deus, muita ajudas, né, como as pessoa [da comunidade dela] via, né, a correria, a nossa correia, assim, falava: "olha Dandara, João, tem um curso ali!"... já vai eu e colocava Tereza e o Gabriel [outro filho], entendeu. A gente deu esse apoio mesmo: "você tem que estudar!"
[25] "Onde branco entra, você entra também".
[26] "Essa oportunidade eu dei mesmo, né, pros meus filhos. Eu não queria que ela [Tereza] passasse, assim, como eu passei".

our family"[27], she reflects. Dandara recalls that they used to give Tereza a book at the end of every school year:

[Tereza] is now finishing her doctorate and I always say: at the end of the school year we [herself and her husband], on birthdays ... I – or my husband – didn't give her a doll, it was a book [that they gave her]. It was a book. I told my husband, I told him, look, João, we gave her so many books that now [Dandara laughs an emotional laugh] Tereza has her own book. My daughter has a [published] book[28]. (Dandara)

Now that Dandara is at a mature stage of her life and her children are adults, she can cherish her daughter's achievements. She highlighted that Tereza has recently fulfilled her lifelong dream of being a mother herself. This only happened now that Tereza is in her forties. Dandara thinks this was the last major event that was missing in her daughter's life – to have a child of her own. About that, she told me:

It's never-ending, right. There is no end ... like ... each moment is a surprise [a good one]. What was missing to her ... she was a well-travelled child, thanks to God, right ... and now comes my little one, right, Carolina. Because Tereza is also a doula. I was very emotional that she [Tereza] had a natural birth, that the birth was here, in my home, where she had the baby, right. That is what was missing. I told Tereza, Tereza, that is the only thing that you were missing: to be a mother, which was a big dream of hers, right, to be a mummy[29]. (Dandara)

---

[27] "A grande faculdade da vida é na casa ... é nóis, é minha familia".
[28] "[Tereza] tá terminando o doutorado dela e, eu sempre falo mesmo: nós aqui, quando passava de ano, aniversário ... não era uma boneca que eu dava – nem meu marido – era um livro. Era um livro. Eu falei assim pro meu marido, eu falei assim: nossa, Luiz, a gente dava tanto livro que hoje a Tereza [começa a rir emocionada] tem livro, né! Tem livro a minha filha."
[29] Não tem fim, né. Não tem fim ... assim ... é cada momento a surpresa. O que faltava pra ela ... foi uma menina viajada, graças a deus, né ... e agora vem a minha caçulinha, né, a Carolina. Porque a Tereza também é doula. E eu fiquei muito emocionada também que foi normal [o parto da filha], que foi aqui na minha casa, que teve [o bebê], né. É isso que faltava. Eu falei assim pra Tereza: "Tereza, era só isso que faltava pra você: ser mãe", que é o grande sonho dela, né, ser mamãe.

1.3 Val

Val is a domestic worker in Campinas (São Paulo) and has been working for the same family for thirty-two years. She told me that she had to change the way she works during the pandemic because her employers are elderly and at high risk of dying of Covid-19. She has been living at work for twenty days, followed by fifteen days at her own home, since July 2020. This increase of unpaid care work, it has been noted, occurred more broadly since the onset of the pandemic (United Nations, 2020). Val's wage has not changed since the new work routine started. She has to put her life on hold while living at her employer's house: she cannot see her boyfriend or daughter, or go to medical appointments as all personal commitments can only take place when she is at her own home. She also had to leave a second job she had one day a week due to the employers also being elderly, and at greater risk of catching the virus if she worked in several households.

Val was born and raised in a small rural property owned by her parents in a remote location in Paraná, in the south of the country. She and her eight siblings worked on the family's land planting beans, corn, rice and cotton, and milking the cows. Her father was against women receiving education – "we were forbidden to study"[30], she says. Unlike her brothers, he did not allow his daughters to study further after they finished primary education; "we paid a high price for that"[31], she reflects. Val left her parent's home against her father's will when she was nineteen years old and migrated with her boyfriend to Campinas: "I moved away without my father's consent; I disobeyed my father"[32], she says.

The migration of the women farmers from their small, family-run, rural properties to a big city in Brazil often comes with the loss of their social identity – a "social death" of the land worker (Silva et al., 2016, p. 2) replaced by a new urban identity in formation. Val struggled to adapt in Campinas: "I did all the farm work, but I didn't do the house chores which

---

[30] "Ele não deixava a gente estudar".
[31] "Pagamos caro por isso".
[32] "Eu vim sem ele querer, mesmo, eu desobedeci meu pai".

is now what I do for a living; I didn't wash, I didn't do the ironing, I didn't cook"*33*. She told me that, in the beginning, she had few domestic skills:

I knew how to clean the dishes; everyone knows how to do it! I also knew how to clean floors – there's nothing to learn about cleaning floors, it's easy to learn. But there are other things that I learned while at work [as a domestic worker]"[34]. (Val)

And she learned new ones:

Now I can say that I can cook ... my employer taught me how to do the ironing as well. I didn't know how to do it – ironing requires some skills that have to be learned[35]. (Val)

The lack of good quality formal education in her rural home town was a source of insecurity when she was younger and moved to the city. She felt less cultured than other people: "I didn't understand many of the conversations I heard people having around me"[36], she said. She struggled to engage in conversations and had difficulty speaking Portuguese, her native language, "correctly" – "even today I can't speak Portuguese properly, but I know I have improved"[37], she told me.

Val met her ex-husband in Campinas and they had a child, Paula. I interviewed Paula, her only child. Her daughter accompanied her to work until she was two years old. After that Paula was sent to a full-time nursery paid for by her mother, as her employer's house had staircases and was not safe for a little child, she told me. I enquired about her ex-husband, and she told me that he was not mentioned in our previous conversations because he never helped financially. Also, she told me, she was abused by him and left him after three years together. She sent me a picture of herself saying "I will

---

[33] "Eu fazia tudo o serviço de roça, mas não fazia o serviço de casa, que é o que eu faço aqui agora; não lavava, não passava, não cozinhava".
[34] "Eu sabia lavar louça, essas coisas todo mundo sabe! Limpar o chão não tem o que saber, aprende fácil. Mas tem umas coisas que eu aprendi aqui [no trabalho]".
[35] "Agora até que eu sei cozinhar ... minha patroa me ensinou a passar roupa, que eu não sabia, que é uma coisa que tem que aprender".
[36] "Não sabia sobre muitas coisas que as pessoas falavam".
[37] "até hoje eu não sei falar direito português bem, mas eu melhorei".

send you a picture of myself ... only so you can see that I am pretty"[38], implying that I would imagine her to be ugly.

Val told me that domestic workers like herself are "invisible" and that domestic work has no value. She corrected herself straight away saying that "other people" see people like her as invisible and "other people" do not value her work and think that "the person that cleans bathrooms and cleans floors only does that because they are incapable of doing anything else"[39]. It is unclear to me if she agrees with "other people" or, perhaps, if she is silently resisting this social categorization. That is the main reason she encouraged her daughter to go to university: she wanted her daughter's work to be recognized: "I wanted her [her daughter] to be someone; I didn't want her to be a simple servant"[40], she says.

Val caught up with secondary education in the evenings when she was an adult and attended a course to be a receptionist. She timidly mentioned that she dreamed of doing a professional college course after finishing secondary education, but had to dismiss it because she was too busy working long hours. She also reflected that she could have pursued a different career, but opted to stay at her job otherwise she would not be able to support her daughter to go to university:

I attended a course that qualified me to work as a hotel receptionist. I had the chance to work in other jobs, to stop being a paid domestic worker and work in reception or in a shop, but I refused to leave my job as I thought to myself, I have stability here; they won't send me away and I can guarantee that she [her daughter Paula] will go to university. I had to have a wage that allowed her to do that [to cover her daughter's university fees] otherwise, it wouldn't be worth starting it [university][41]. (Val)

---

[38] "Eu vou mandar uma foto minha pra você ... só pra você ver que eu sou bonita".
[39] "a pessoa que faz isso, que lava o banheiro, que limpa o chão, ela faz isso porque ela não sabe fazer outra coisa".
[40] "queria que ela fosse alguém e não uma simples serviçal".
[41] "Eu fiz um curso de recepcionista em hotel, eu tive chance de trabalhar, de sair de doméstica e trabalhar tipo em recepção ou em loja, mas só que eu não saía, porque eu falava assim: 'aqui eu tô garantida, eles não vão me mandar embora, e eu tô garantida para ela [Paula] fazer a faculdade'. Eu tinha que ter um salário que garantisse, senão não adiantava começar".

Val's employers paid part of Paula's university fees. She told me that without their support it would be unlikely that Paula would have gone to university as she studied in a private institution and had to pay expensive tuition fees. Nevertheless, Val paid for most of her daughter's studies: part of the university fees, books and materials, food and transport, she listed. She remembers that she had to work more hours and save money to support Paula at university:

> *She'd go to university no matter what, even if that meant that I'd have to stop buying things for myself. I was renting at that time – nowadays I have my own place – so there were many things that I couldn't afford to purchase: if I couldn't afford them I just couldn't [have them]! I couldn't afford to see my mother during that time as she lived far away, and it cost money to travel to see her ... no trips to see mother then! There will be no trips: I will use the money to pay for my daughter's university fees instead. She [her daughter Paula] didn't enter university through the quota system and she wasn't helped by anybody else but me ... and her strong will to pursue her studies.*[42] (Val)

I learned from my conversation with Paula, Val's daughter, that she did not live with Val when she was a child. Val did not mention that in our conversations, and I had to ask her further about it after speaking to Paula. Val explained me that she "forgot" to mention that her daughter did not live with her from the age of six until she was thirteen years old. She lived with her father and grandparents instead.

Val told me that when Paula reached six years old and went to primary school she struggled with childcare as there was no free full-time education available, and she was a single woman with a full-time job. Even if she could afford any sort of childcare after school hours, she would not be able to take her daughter to childcare because she would not be able to leave work to collect her daughter from school. As a migrant woman, she could

---

[42] "Ela vai estudar de qualquer jeito, mesmo que eu deixava de comprar as coisas. Eu pagava aluguel na época – hoje não – então tinha umas coisas que não dava pra comprar: não dava, não dava! Não podia viajar para a minha mãe que é em outro estado ... não, não vai viajar: vai pagar a faculdade! Ela [Paula] nunca teve cotas e não foi incentivada por outras pessoas, só por mim e pelo que ela mesmo queria: estudar".

not count on her family's help because they were far away. The restraints led Val to allow her daughter to live with her father and paternal grandparents as her ex-husband moved back to his parents' house after they ended their relationship. Val told me that Paula's grandparents raised her daughter, not her ex-husband: her grandfather was retired and was responsible for the school trips and her grandmother was in charge of Paula's day-to-day care as she worked from home as a seamstress.

Val saw Paula at weekends and provided for food and other needs on a weekly basis, as her ex-husband struggled to keep a job. She was also in charge of the child's medical needs, staying with Paula in hospital when the child had an operation. Val says her daughter expressed her will to move back with her when she was thirteen as she started to have romantic interests and found it difficult to live with her conservative father.

Paula went to private secondary education while back at her mother's home. Val paid for her studies and Paula was granted a partial scholarship after passing a test. Paula obtained a college degree in advertising and marketing, also paid for by her mother. Val told me that her daughter was offered a paid trainee place related to her degree soon after that, and another job opportunity while at university. This time it was in a multinational company, which offered her a permanent job after her graduation and is the place where she has been working since then.

I met Val in person for the first time in 2022 when I was visiting Brazil. She has a very busy life, and we exchanged many messages until we finally met. I met her in the evening, in front of her employer's house. She was dressed in sports clothes and told me she had just came back from a walk. She enjoys walking around the block where her employers live and told me that her employer encourages her to do exercise. Because of his encouragement, she goes for daily walks after or during work time and she also started doing Pilates in a gym. Her employers are an elderly couple and one of them has lost mobility recently, requiring additional care that she has been helping to provide. She is no longer living part-time at her employer's house and told me that she is doing the handover of the additional responsibilities at work to a carer who was hired a few weeks before. She is very close to her employers and wants to make sure the carers looking after them are trustworthy and that they will be in good hands when she is not there. She told me that her plan is to retire and move close to her mother and sisters again, migrating back to the place where she was born and enjoy their company, helping and being helped by them.

1.4 Vitória

Vitória was born and raised in her family's small rural property in a remote location in Ceará in the northeast of the country. "It is cruel there"[43], Vitória says as she describes her home town in the northeastern backlands. Her family was very poor, and she and her siblings had to walk seven kilometres on foot to school when they were little as the school was in a nearby village. Her parents needed their children to help working their land and all siblings ended up leaving school early due to that. Vitória left school before finishing primary education.

Acute poverty and the lack of opportunities in Vitória's home town led her to move to the southeast of the country. She migrated to Campinas when she was twenty-one years old and had to leave her one-year-old daughter Claudia behind. The child was raised by Vitória's parents as she had no means to look after her with the prospect of working full-time and having no accommodation secured in the new city. Her first job was as domestic worker and she lived at her employers' house, as she could not afford to live elsewhere.

Vitória told me she worked from six in the morning until ten or sometimes eleven o'clock in the evening. Her employers did not pay overtime and her wage was below the minimum wage. She worked for a couple with three young children. The family lived in the city but they were farmers, managing the people who worked their land elsewhere. The employer "was very suspicious of other people"[44] she said, and searched her belongings on a regular basis behind her back, looking for stolen items in her bedroom and handbag. Vitória recalls that she noticed her handbag and drawers were searched and complained about it to her employer. The employer blamed the children, saying it was likely the little girl had played with her belongings. Vitória did not trust the explanation, and after that she started to lock her room before leaving the house on her days off, on Sundays. Her employer immediately noticed that the room was locked. She

---

[43] "Lá é cruel".
[44] "era muito desconfiada".

was so angry with Vitória's attitude that she stalked her in her car when Vitória left the house on foot, and demanded that she handed over the keys. She was shouting at Vitória, without stopping the car. "I don't like to talk about it because I get so nervous it makes me shiver"[45], Vitória says. "I felt like rubbish, you know? I was feeling humiliated"[46], she adds.

When I meet Vitória in person in 2022, she told me that years later, the former employer keeps stalking her in her car. The place where Vitória works is very close to her previous employer's home, on the same street. When Vitória is walking her employer's dog or walking from work to the bus stop, her previous employer would follow her with her car and, recently she lost control of the car, almost hitting Vitória and the dog she had with her. The car was driven towards her, and she fell down on the kerb. The previous employer came to her current employer's house after that. Vitória said her former employer wanted to apologize and said that she did not mean to hit her or hurt her, that it was an honest accident. Vitória thinks she only came to see her because she was concerned that Vitória would call the police. Vitória was very nervous when telling me about this episode and said that she has no doubts that the woman tried to hurt her, or worse. Despite that she did not call the police, afraid she would not be able to prove what had happened. Vitória told me that the ex-employer recently put her family house up for sale, and they moved away to a new home elsewhere. She is relieved as she thinks the stalking is likely to stop now that she is finally at a safe distance from her previous employer.

Vitória has many stories from when she worked at her ex-employer's home. She told me about a letter she wrote to her father who lives in Ceará, and asked her employer to post for her. She found the letter opened in her employers' car glovebox compartment more than two months later: "every time I remember that it makes me so angry, I wish I could hit her [her employer] in the face"[47], she says. She rescued her letter without mentioning it to her employer and posted it herself.

After three years working for this family Vitória asked to leave, counting on a new job she found through her sister. Her employer did not accept it well and started arguing, shouting at her, banging and kicking doors after

---

[45] "Não gosto nem de falar essas coisas porque eu fico até tremendo de nervoso".
[46] "Fui me sentindo assim um lixo, sabe? Eu fui me sentindo humilhada".
[47] "quando eu me lembro me dá uma raiva, me dá vontade de dar na cara dela".

leaving the room. "If I'd let down my guard, she would probably have hit me"[48], she recalls. Her employer made her husband speak to Vitória to persuade her to stay. Vitória told him her decision was final but did not tell him her reasons: "I didn't tell him about my thoughts ... these people believe themselves to be powerful, they think they are better than us so it would be a waste [of time] to tell him how I felt"[49]. Vitória told her employer that her new employer would pick her up by car, but she was against it. Instead, she forced Vitória into her car and told her "I will drive you to your brother's home just like I did when you first arrived from the northeast, and I collected you from there"[50]. Vitória was not able to speak to her new employer about the change of plans and they were unable to meet as she was prevented from showing up: "when I recall that moment, I feel this anguish inside me"[51], Vitória says.

Vitória has worked for two other families since this first job and has been in the last one for twenty-seven years. She has a good relationship with her current employer and a formal job, earning more than the minimum national wage and receiving payment accordingly when working overtime. She had a second daughter, Helena. I interviewed Helena.

I was not originally planning to consider stories of daughters of domestic workers that did not go to university but, after interviewing Vitória, I decided to include a brief story of her other daughter, Claudia, as her dissonant trajectory compared to the other daughter's path is highly relevant in Vitória's life story. I did not interview Claudia; all information I have is based on Vitória's narrative.

Vitória recalls that "I was father and mother at the same time"[52] when Claudia was little, without giving further details about the father of her child. She sent money to her mother every month to raise Claudia after moving to Campinas. She had contact with her daughter via telephone, mostly through her mother and visited her one year after she left, followed by a second visit four years later and two other following trips.

---

[48] "Se eu tivesse dado bobeira eu tinha apanhado dela".
[49] "não vou ficar falando ... esse povo é poderoso, acha que pode mais do que a gente, então não vou nem falar".
[50] "eu vou levar você na casa do seu irmão do jeitinho que eu te busquei no dia que você chegou de viagem".
[51] "quando eu me lembro me dá até uma angústia por dentro".
[52] "eu era pai e mãe ao mesmo tempo".

She says Claudia had many problems and was a difficult child at school. Vitória was once contacted by phone by the schoolteacher to discuss her daughter's troubled school life but, impotent to act upon it, she replied: "I know how difficult it is ... but I can't do anything about it"[53], because of her being such a distance away. Things escalated and Vitória's mother gave up sending Claudia to school when she was fourteen years old. "She is useless because she didn't study"[54], Vitória says about her daughter. Claudia left school earlier than her mother did. She moved in with her boyfriend when she was fifteen years old, and they had two children. Vitória struggles to remember the age of her grandchildren and says that she last saw them three years ago when she last visited Ceará. Claudia has recently given birth to her third child – coincidentally, in the same month Helena had her first baby.

Vitória has a close relationship with Helena's child, and mother and daughter have a very different relationship compared to the one Vitória has with her eldest. The mother says she prefers not to have contact with Claudia because she is rude and rebellious. She speaks about Claudia bitterly: "[Claudia] is in this situation because she didn't think properly, she didn't do things right ... she could have been a different person, but she preferred to choose things to be as they are so ... what can we do about it?"[55] and often compares her two daughters showing a meritocratic approach.

Vitória told me that she paid for Helena's university tuition fees and has been providing further financial aid since Helena left home as her daughter struggles to make ends meet with her wage of a primary school teacher. Claudia, on the other hand, receives no support and is trapped in the same challenging environment that her mother experienced herself – and escaped from – experiencing all sorts of deprivations.

---

[53] "eu sei que está difícil ... mas eu não posso fazer nada".
[54] "Ela não serve pra nada porque ela não tem um nada de estudo".
[55] "[Claudia] está nessa situação porque ela não pensou, não fez as coisas direito ... podia ter sido outra pessoa, mas quis escolher essa situação, então ... o que vai fazer?".

1.5 Carmem

Carmem told me she married young, but it is unclear if she regrets that. She adds that getting married and having children before going to university had an impact on her financial autonomy. She got married when she was eighteen years old, soon after finishing secondary education, and had two children. She was a full-time mother until her younger child, Julia reached ten years old. I interviewed Julia. The mother recalls:

> *I was very young when I married, right, I got married when I was eighteen years old. And, like, I finish secondary school when I was seventeen years old ... I finished secondary school and when I was already eighteen years old, I got married: I started dating my husband when I was seventeen, and I was already married by the time I was eighteen years old. Then, after two years of marriage I was a mother already. So, I stayed ... I stayed some time only dedicating myself to my daughter, right. When I resumed to my work my daughter was already ten years old; I had her already and I also had my son, Marcus*[56]. (Carmem)

Carmem had to interrupt her studies and was unable to start a career of her own as she was looking after her children. When I asked her what life opportunities she wished her daughter had that she did not have herself, she told me that she wished that her daughter had continued her education – and she had the opportunity to do it. She says:

> *I wished hard that she didn't stop her studies; that she searched for more knowledge ... because I was only able to catch up with my studies, to have a higher education degree, after they [her children] were adults, right. I finished university when ... I was forty-seven years of age. But, anyways, it all ended up well, I finished it [her course] ... I LOVE the course I did which is cookery*[57]. (Carmem)

---

[56] "Eu casei muito cedo, né, eu casei com dezoito anos de idade. E, assim, eu terminei o ensino médio quando eu tava com dezessete anos ... eu terminei o ensino médio e com 18 já casei: comecei a namorá meu marido com dezessete, com dezoito anos já casei. Aí com dois anos de casado já fui mãe. Entao eu fiquei ... eu fiquei um tempo só me dedicando a minha filha, né. Quando eu voltei a trabalhar, minha filha já tava com dez anos de idade; eu já tinha ela e já tinha também o meu filho, o Marcus".
[57] "Eu gostaria muito que ela não parasse de estudar; que ela busque mais conhecimentos ... porque eu só pude voltar a estudar, concluir a faculdade, depois

Carmem has previously worked as a cook at nurseries and schools and as a shop assistant. She worked in a hospital for four years after attending a course to be a radiology technician, but left the job as she was unhappy working in the health sector. More recently, she worked as a domestic worker for a family in Campinas for almost eight years and has a good relationship with her former employers. There she had a formal job and worked regular hours, but she decided to leave as she was offered work in a hotel after obtaining a professional degree that qualified her to design meals for diabetics. She told me:

It took me some time to come back [to catch up with her studies] because of [my] financial situation, right, and because ... the other jobs I had wouldn't allow me to have flexible time, right. But then, after I started to work at Juliana [her employer when she was a domestic worker], as I started work at 9am and left at 5pm, that allowed me to have more flexible time and, due to that, I was able to catch up with my studies and to conclude my university course[58]. (Carmem)

Carmem is the only mother I interviewed who had obtained a university degree: Carmem studied cookery, when she was forty-seven years old. Her daughter obtained her degree before her mother and Julia was the first woman in her family to have one. When I asked her about her mother's life opportunities, Carmem said: "unfortunately, my mother didn't have the conditions to go to university[59]".

Carmem strongly believes in education as a means for a better life:

the knowledge, the studies that we obtain along the years ... that can't be taken away from us: this stays forever ... if you don't have ... you don't necessarily have to have a university degree, but if you don't have some

---

deles já grande, né. Fui terminar a faculdade já com ... quarenta e sete anos de idade. Mas, enfim, deu tudo certo, eu concluí ... eu AMO faculdade que eu fiz, que é de gastronomia".
[58] "Eu demorei pra voltar, por condições financeiras, né, e por ... os outros trabalho que eu trabalhava que não me permitiam um horário flexível, né. Mas aí, depois que eu fui trabalhá na Juliana, como eu entrava às 9 da manhã e saía às 5 da tarde, aí já foi um horário mais flexível e aí deu pra eu voltá a estudá e concluí a faculdade".
[59] "Infelizmente a minha mãe ela não teve condições de ir pra uma faculdade".

knowledge, right, about how to behave in places, how to debate certain topics, you end up kind of being left behind[60]. (Carmem)

She told me that she was not able to support Julia to pay for her professional degree in beauty but helped her in other ways. She said:

My daughter had my full support, since the first university course she had started, but she didn't like, but I've always supported her … Financially, I could do very little to help but I did all within my means to support her. But I gave her loads of moral support, I even helped her to do her university work[61]. (Carmem)

The driving force behind Carmem's efforts to help her daughter to go to university was that her daughter followed a different path from herself, pursuing financial independency rather than becoming a housewife and mother at a young age: "[I] always supported her [to go to university], right, because I wanted … I didn't want her to be a simple housewife and mother, right, so she would have more knowledge, right, to be independent, to have her own space, right"[62].

Carmem experienced at first hand the benefits of having a university degree as that allowed her to quickly leave behind her job as domestic worker and do what she really wanted: to work preparing specialised meals in a hotel. However, also very importantly, she saw the benefits of having a degree by following the life trajectory of her son (her older child). That served as an example for herself and Julia, inspiring thoughts of new paths for the family.

---

[60] "o conhecimento, os estudos que a gente adquire com o tempo ... isso ninguém tira, né: isso fica pra sempre ... se você não tiver ... não digo uma faculdade, mas um conhecimento, né, saber se comportar nos lugares a falar, a debater certos assuntos, você acaba meio que ficando pra trás".

[61] "Minha filha teve o meu apoio total, desde a primeira faculdade que ela começô, mas ela não gostô, mas sempre apoiei ... Financeiramente eu não pude apoiá muito, mas no pouco que dava pra eu ajuda, eu ajudava. Mas dava muito apoio moral, até ajudava ela fazê os trabalhos da faculdade".

[62] "[Eu] apoiei sempre, né, pois eu queria ... eu não queria que ela fosse apenas uma dona de casa e mãe, né, pra ela ter mais conhecimentos, né, ser independente, tê o espaço dela, né".

According to the person who introduced me to Carmem, her son helped her to pay for her university degree himself. Carmem did not mention that in our conversations, but she mentioned her son and told me more about his role on Julia's education:

> Partly, what helped her [Julia] to enter [university] was her own efforts, right, because she started to work early, when she was fourteen years old ... and it was also the family's encouragement, mainly from her brother, Marcus, who has a degree in pharmacy, works in a very good multinational corporation, at Boehringer. He has a higher education degree, a post-graduation degree as well; he speaks four languages fluently, thank God he is good, he already lives by himself in Sao Paulo, has his own life. And he was the one who encouraged [Julia] the most, also, at that time, [encouraged] her to study, to go to university[63]. (Carmem)

1.6 Findings

The domestic workers I interviewed experienced different types of trauma, mostly related to acute poverty, including abuse and exploitation at work. One of them was stalked by a previous employer who did not stop when she left the job, culminating in a situation that put her life at risk when her ex-employer lost control of the car – or, allegedly, did it on purpose – and drove towards her when she was walking her employers' dog. They were silenced by different forms of oppression but all of them nevertheless challenged these conditions both at a personal level and through their daughters.

All mothers experienced deprivation of basic needs, greatly affecting their education and childhood as they started working early in life to contribute to their family's income. Most women notably prioritized the little spare money they earned working as domestic workers and school cleaners to spend on education for their children, as Dandara, Val, Vitória

---

[63] "Em parte o que mais ajudou [a entrar na faculdade] foi o esforço próprio dela, né, que ela começo a trabalhar cedo, aos quatorze anos ... e também foi a motivação da família, principalmente do irmão Marcus, que já é formado em farmácia, trabalha numa empresa multinacional muito boa, na Bochringer. Ele já é formado, pós graduado; fala quatro idiomas fluentememte, graças a deus tá bem, já mora sozinho em São Paulo, tem a vida própria dele. E ele foi o maior incentivador, também, na época, pra ela estuda, fazê faculdade".

and Marilla did. Many worked longer hours to afford that, and it was only possible when they had a formal job and their employers paid them the national minimum wage and for the additional hours they worked. All but one of them tried to catch up with their own studies later in life, but working long hours combined with the need to provide for their daughters' education made it difficult for them to pursue their own ambitions, which would eventually lead to a change in their occupation and social status. Val consciously dismissed her plans of pursuing a professional degree and becoming a receptionist after qualifying for it, as her employers offered to pay part of her daughter's university fees. Leaving her job at that moment would have jeopardized Paula's higher education and she opted to stay at her job to benefit her daughter.

Marilla lost all of her teeth due to the lack of opportunity to have them properly treated while she was still young, and, according to her daughter, became bitter and depressed with time. Despite that, she pursued a steady job as a cleaner in a Court of Justice, passed the tests, and the increased wage was used to pay for her daughter's English lessons and a one-year preparatory course that led her to a top public university. Although Vitória was unable to change careers, she managed to change jobs and improved her life after suffering abuse and exploitation in her first job as a domestic worker. After migrating from the northeast to the southeast, her wages and additional pay working on Saturdays allowed her to pay for her daughter's university fees and provided further financial aid when Helena left the family home. She showed tremendous agency resisting her ex-employer's abuse by locking her room, refusing to be searched, rescuing her letter from her employer's car and ultimately by leaving her job, despite being intimidated to stay.

Val wants to be seen and sent me a picture of herself. She was silenced early in life by patriarchy, by her father's sexist view against women being educated. This literally silenced her later in life when she migrated from her rural home town to a big city and learned that she was unable to speak her own mother tongue "properly", so struggling to engage in conversations. The same forces of *machismo* were present in her first marriage as she was abused by her ex-husband. Carmem felt similar forces as she was unable to pursue a career when she was a young, full-time mother; pursuing it later in life allowed her to leave her position as a paid domestic worker to enter the world of professional cooking.

Knowing briefly about Carmem's son's trajectory, I had a glimpse on how the widening access to higher education in the country also benefited young men and how this turned into a virtuous cycle within families, inspiring a collective pursuit of education and creating role models within families and beyond. The birth of first-generation university entrants came along with the creation of a collective imaginary that saw higher education as a real possibility for the first time, no matter a person's social origin.

All mothers were highly committed to their jobs as some were the "head" in their families while others had a substantial participation in the family's income. Among other things, they needed to finance their children's studies, either to keep their children out of work when they were at school like Dandara did, or to pay for their daughter's university tuition fees like Vitória and Val. Because of that, all daughters but one did not experience working from an early age and none had to stop their education before finishing primary education as many mothers had. Only one of the daughters I interviewed left school before finishing secondary education when she was sixteen, but she was able to catch up and enter university, nonetheless. They were poor, but unlike their mothers, they did not experience acute poverty.

Some domestic workers have also experienced restricted forms of social mobility themselves, as some left their rural home towns for big cities and were able to achieve a stable career by working in the same household for many years like Vitória and Val, or achieving stability after passing a test to become a professional cleaner in a public office, like Marília did. With time, some were able to build or purchase their own homes and to provide financial aid to their teenage and adult daughters, an improvement from the early childhood experiences of deprivation their children and they have experienced.

The better life of the daughters was possible because their mothers spent longer hours as domestic workers and they coped with difficult conditions. However, all the difficult conditions often forced these mothers to be absent from their children's lives, sometimes from the early days. Some mothers took their children with them to work before they were at school age, as they struggled with childcare. Some who are migrating women faced additional difficulties with childcare, without the supporting network of their families to help. Those who were able to be present at home, like Carmem as she experienced being a full-time mother, did it at the cost of their financial autonomy and at the expense of their own educational ambitions that were only able to be pursued later in life.

A couple of women also had their voices silenced as mothers: Vitória had to leave her baby behind in the northeast, estranging their relationship, while Val had to separate herself from her daughter for many years as she had to work full-time and could not afford childcare alone. Conflicts between the rural and urban worlds also helped in making Val voiceless as her farming skills were of no use when she moved to Campinas. That made her feel invisible and unvalued by others. The invisibilization of their work – paid and unpaid – awoke a strong desire in these mothers to help their daughters to pursue higher education as a form of escaping from being a "simple" servant, as Val said, or a "simple housewife and mother" as mentioned by Carmem.

When asked about what they wished for her daughters after they obtained a degree, they often started their sentences saying, "I wished/I wanted" but they would quickly rephrase it to "I didn't want her to …". The mothers' narratives showed me that decisions of investing resources in their children's formal education were often taken not because of the great expectations they had about the outcome of a degree – they did not know what that outcome would be as they never had one themselves, or had role models in their families before them – but because of what they knew. Because of what they knew and what they could relate themselves to, they did not want their daughters to experience the same things they did and have undignified work conditions and difficult lives. A university degree would spare them from that, the mothers believed.

Although the mothers I interviewed are invisibilized to society, their voices and life stories have had an incredible strength in their daughter's realm, even if they were unable to be more physically present in their lives. In most cases these motherly voices had a positive tone, while in others, they were daunting and left emotional scars on the daughters I interviewed. Nevertheless, they were rather powerful in driving their daughters to a different path towards social mobility, as I will explore further in the next chapter.

Chapter Two

A Job to Read and Write (The Daughters)

Employment Officer: *Would you like to work in an office? Or would you prefer manual work?*
Billy: *What's that, manual work?*
Employment Officer: *It means working with your hands, for example, building, farming, engineering. Jobs like that, as opposed to pen-pushing jobs.*
Billy: *I'd be all right working in an office, wouldn't I? I've a job to read and write.*

Dialogue at the Youth Employment Meeting (Hines, 2000)

According to Stuart (2012), higher education has an important role to provide young people from working-class backgrounds the ability to move into professional occupations after obtaining a degree. In Brazil, 21.5% of women and 15.6% of men have a university degree but although women have 37.9% more degrees than men, black women are 2.3 times behind white women and 10% behind white men that obtained one (IBGE, 2018). Also, the same studies show that despite more women having higher education degrees, there is a gap between qualification and income in the job market as women's wages were 63.4% of their male counterparts from 2012-2016.

Many NGOs have been advocating for women's economic empowerment, defined by the Bill & Melinda Gates Foundation as:

> the transformative process that helps women and girls move from limited power, voice and choice at home and in the economy to having the skills,

resources, and opportunities needed to compete equitably in markets as well as the agency to control and benefit from economic gains[64].

The Foundation's case study about Brazil shows that the country's government policies focused on care work produced a meaningful increase in women's labour force participation during the early 2000s. These policies included free day-care programmes for children aged from birth to six years old and improved parental leave, as well as expanding education combined with national economic growth (Gates Foundation, 2017).

Women's economic empowerment is especially important for black and northeastern women in Brazil, as racial bias and regional prejudice against these groups makes them more vulnerable to discrimination and violence (Batista et al., 2014; Magalhães, 2015). Empowerment of these women through higher education allows them to challenge the stereotypical images they have, created by the intersecting oppressions of classism, racism and sexism. It has an important role towards the construction of self-love and social representativity – both needed to redefine imaginaries in Brazil and indeed, everywhere.

The mothers and daughters I interviewed experienced these progressive years that empowered women in Brazil. The daughters obtained a university degree during this period and were the first generation of women in their families to have one. They have all achieved better social status compared to their parents. Empowerment also had an important role in the experience and resolution of trauma suffered by these women, as they are highly affected by the levels of oppression in their life. Bettering lives after breaking the cycle of paid domestic work among women in their families after obtaining a university degree benefited their mental health and abilities to access the help they need, for themselves and for their families.

The mainstream narratives exploring the recent upturn in numbers of young, working-class women attending university in Brazil overlook and silence the strength of mothers of this new generation, contributing to invisibilizing the role of these women. The parental role in this process is often erased and shadowed by the government's affirmative action policies

---

[64] https://www.gatesfoundation.org/equal-is-greater/our-approach [accessed 21/02/2023]

or by the romantization of personal efforts of the first-generation university entrants in a meritocratic, individual-based approach.

The state overtaking the role of families during times of social welfare programmes is not new. In his book *The Maternalists* (2021), Bar-Haim explores the relationship of the British welfare state and the gendered figure of a "nanny state" after the Second World War. He argues that a new mother-centred culture shaped the welfare state itself. Based on the Carolyn Steedman memoir *What My Mother Lacked, I Was Given*, he argues that the British state intervention acted as a parental surrogate with caring responsibilities. Although Brazil lacks the experience of a welfare state as formerly seen in countries of the global north, the active role of the government in widening access to higher education in the early 2000s created a similar collective imaginary described by Bar-Haim, where the state was perceived as having a parental role in people's lives. The state became a place to project feelings such as hate and hostility (of those against the affirmative action policies) as well as gratitude (of those who benefited or were in favour). Indeed, as the state was committed to a more equalitarian access to higher education; the first-generation university entrants were "given" what their parents lacked. However, when this massive expansion in higher education is fully explained by government policies, it removes agency from the families of these first-generation university entrants and the roles they had in their children's pursuit of a place at university. My interviews showed that families, especially mothers, had an active and key role breaking the vicious cycle of intergenerational inequality within their families by prioritizing their children's education, often at the cost of their own education and ambitions.

All of the first-generation university entrants I interviewed are skilled workers now and their occupations are related to their degrees. Most of these women have higher incomes than the previous generation, based on what I could gather from their life stories, as well as better social status, compared to their parents. However, they carry the weight of being the first in their families to obtain a degree and are in the process of seeking social respectability (Skeggs, 2002). As such, they often face pressures that their peers who are not first-generation university entrants did not, before and after obtaining a university degree.

It was not uncommon for the first-generation university entrants, like their mothers, to have also had experiences of trauma in the early years as they had their care giving disrupted in different ways. These daughters experienced trauma because of their social context, a combination of poverty and failures of government providing quality public education; one of the women I interviewed also experienced discrimination and racism from an early age as a black woman.

When I spoke to mothers and daughters, all women showed a strong sense of responsibility for caring and providing for their children. Often the conditions and resources that allowed their daughters to focus on their education was provided only by their "strong" mothers. Likewise, the daughters showed incredible resilience in the pursuit of education, experiencing very unfavourable conditions to study and thrive, despite their family's support.

According to Moeller, women from developing nations carry the weight of being "always responsible for more than herself" (2018, p. 96). In her book, Moeller explores how large corporations, with the support of governments and NGOs, created the idea of investing in girls to end poverty – the "girl effect" theory (Hengeveld, 2015; Moeller, 2018). Rather than tackling human rights issues and issues that fuel poverty and gender stereotypes, such programmes investing in poor, racialized girls became a "business case" for large corporations: instead of investing in girls to end poverty, they invest in their potential market value, as "there are profits to be made at the bottom of this pyramid" (Moeller, 2018, p. 199). It is profitable to naturalize the idea that these "wonder women" are the only hope for the future. Such a mindset eventually makes many women feel empowered to pursue their objectives but often, the pressure to thrive in the most adverse conditions and do better than men is a heavy weight and a source of anxiety in their lives.

In this chapter, I will explore how the daughters of domestic workers thrived, all facing very challenging contexts to gain access to higher education. I will investigate the family environment that gave them a choice that was lacking for their mothers: the choice of "a job to read and write". Similar to their mother's life stories in the previous chapter, some are deeper and richer in details while others are restricted, based on what I gathered in my interviews.

2.1 Lucia

Lucia and her brother accompanied their mother Marilla to work from when she was four years old until she turned six and started school. Her mother's work shift as a school cleaner was from two o'clock in the afternoon until eleven in the evening and she had to carry Lucia back home as the child was exhausted by that time. Lucia told me she remembers that her mother had to walk up a ramp to reach their house from the bus stop, carrying her in her arms when they arrived from her mother's work, around midnight.

Lucia helped her mother cleaning desks and gathering dirt from the floor at the school where Marilla worked. When she finished helping her mother, she spent the rest of her time at the school library. "My passion for books, literature and narratives in general might have started there, in this very unlikely context"[65], she says.

The family was poor, and that made Lucia feel insecure about herself when she was younger. She said that only later in life did she understand those feelings. She told me that she used to dress herself very boyish when younger, in times she wanted to feel stronger: "[…] many of my clothes were second-handed from my cousins, I often wore boys' clothes […] I was very much like … very boyish, sometimes, you know, to feel myself stronger"[66].

As the younger sibling, Lucia followed her older siblings' steps and left her parents' home in Itapecerica da Serra (São Paulo) to go to college in São Paulo, determined to pursue a professional degree and enter the job market quickly. "I lacked parameters at home […] but I knew I wouldn't be like my parents"[67], she recalls. She struggled with a low self-esteem: "I had a very low self-esteem […] now I understand that it had a lot to do with my social position"[68] and she was frustrated with her choice of studies. She began to

---

[65] "Minha paixão por livros, literatura e narrativas em geral deve ter começado aí, num contexto um tanto improvável".
[66] "[...] tem muita roupa que eu usava que era de primo, usava sempre muita roupa masculina ...] eu tinha uma coisa de ser muito ... até de me masculinizar, às vezes, sabe, pra se sentir um pouco mais forte".
[67] "Eu não tinha muito parâmetro ... eu sabia que eu não ia ser igual meus pais".
[68] "eu tinha uma auto estima muito baixa [...] hoje eu sei que tem muito a ver com a questão social".

develop motivation to pursue an academic degree and decided to apply for a place on a languages and literature programme at university. She started a one-year preparatory course to pass the university exams, funded by her mother. Around the same time, she started having English lessons on Saturdays, also paid for by Marilla, and was promised a job as an English teacher by her English school if she passed the university exams to study languages and literature. No-one in her family had an academic degree – her older siblings had professional ones – and Lucia told me that her mother wanted her to become a civil servant instead: "since I was eighteen years old my mother has been telling me to pass the tests and become a civil servant"[69], she says.

Lucia passed the university entrance exams at her first attempt and studied languages and literature at one of the most prestigious universities in Brazil, the University of São Paulo (USP). She is the only daughter I interviewed that did her undergraduate studies in a public university. She did not benefit from the governmental programmes for higher education and told me that she would probably never have been offered a place without her family's support: "I had my family's support to enter university ... I would never be able to pass the university entrance exams without the private preparatory course I did [paid by her mother] and without further help I received from them"[70], she says. She added that she also benefited from subsidized meals as she studied in a public university. Lucia is also the only daughter I interviewed that did not live with her parents while at university. Her course was full-time, and she did not to have to pay tuition fees because public universities in Brazil are free of charge. However, she had to work during her studies to pay for her living costs, living in a costly, big city. She found work opportunities at her university and worked on two paid internships while also teaching English privately elsewhere.

Lucia was promised a permanent job by her employer in the university's department she had been working in by the time she finished her degree, but the offer was cancelled at the last moment, close to Christmas Day. Lucia's mental health deteriorated significantly due to that. She told me about how

---

[69] "desde que eu tinha dezoito anos, minha mãe falava para eu fazer concurso público".
[70] "pra eu entrar na universidade eu tive o apoio familiar ... eu não conseguiria jamais se eu não tivesse feito o cursinho e tudo o mais".

frustrated she was seeing herself jobless by the time she graduated. All the expectations she had after all her and her family's efforts did not translate, immediately after graduating, into a good job – or a job at all. She had depression and had to move back to her parents' house:

> *I had this big concern of having to work while doing my studies. I was very afraid of being 'a nobody' in life, the kind of fear of being poor, of being a pauper. It sucks being lower-middle-class as you are moving up in the [social] ladder but, suddenly, if something happens, you go down again. This happened to me twice. I had a more or less dignified job but if I lose it, if I have no support, that source of income is gone, the dream is gone. Despite you sometimes being able to transit through places where other people go, of gaining very symbolic and material accesses, you don't have a backup: if something happens to you ... for example, if you are laid off ... and you don't have a backup, you are screwed. I didn't have anybody paying for my stuff*[71]. (Lucia)

Before the unemployment experience, Lucia was keen to pursue a master's degree. After that, she says, it made her dismiss further academic ambitions: "that was when I decided that having a job was more important"[72], she says. She decided to study to pass a test to become a civil servant and have a steady job, instead of applying for a post-graduate course as she originally wanted. She passed the test and has been working in the same part-time job since then. The steady income and spare time allowed her to have a comfortable life and to pursue other projects including a master's in education at USP, and to provide financial help to her parents. She believes that passing the test for a civil service job is the reason for her social mobility rather than obtaining a university degree.

---

[71] "Eu tinha uma preocupação muito grande de trabalhar e estudar. Eu tinha muito medo de não ser ninguém na vida, esse medo que a gente tem de ser pobre, ser miserável. Porque ser classe média baixa é uma merda, você está ali subindo, mas qualquer coisa, cai tudo. Isso me aconteceu duas vezes. Eu tinha um emprego mais ou menos digno, mas se eu perco ele, se eu não tenho suporte, acabou aquela renda, acabou o sonho. Apesar de você às vezes frequentar os mesmos lugares de outras pessoas, ter acessos bem simbólicos e materiais, você não tem um colchão; se te acontece alguma coisa, como ser demitida, e você não tem um colchão, danou-se. Eu não tinha quem pagasse as coisas pra mim."
[72] "Foi quando eu decidi que o trabalho era mais importante."

Despite Lucia's successful career, Marilla mentioned in our conversation that "what I really dream about"[73] is to see Lucia studying law. "I look at her and I see a lawyer"[74], Marilla said – and asked me to tell that to Lucia when I spoke to her. Lucia told me that she believes her mother wants her to have a profession that gives her social recognition: "she wanted to have a 'doctor' in the family, one that had a profession more valued by society, with more status … [and] she admires people who dress smartly"[75], she says. As pointed out by Skeggs (2002), respectability is one of the most important signifiers of class and "is usually the concern of those who are not seen to have it" (p.1). Lucia said she is not concerned about dressing to impress others. She told me that she recently accompanied her mother to a doctor's appointment and dressed herself "better": "I dressed myself more smartly to make her happy"[76], as she knows this is an issue to her mother and wanted to please her.

2.2 Tereza

Tereza is Dandara's daughter. When I asked her what her motivations were behind her choice of course at university she told me: "I was very keen to have a profession that would prepare me to have the skills to help people that were victims of inequalities such as black people; this was something that has always affected me"[77]. Going to university was a way to do it, according to her. She is the only daughter that told me that she is an activist, and she has been involved with social movements through her church and with black collectives against racism from an early age.

Tereza and her brother accompanied their mother Dandara at work during her first six years of life. Tereza says her early memories are all about leaving home with her mother and brother in the dark, early in the morning,

---

[73] "o meu sonho mesmo."
[74] "Parece que eu vejo ela uma advogada."
[75] "ela queria ter um 'dotô' na família, alguém que fosse de uma profissão mais socialmente valorizada, que tivesse status ... ela admira pessoas que vestem roupa bonita."
[76] "eu até fui um pouco mais arrumadinha pra ela ficar feliz."
[77] "eu queria muito uma profissão que pudesse me ajudar a ter um preparo para colaborar para as pessoas que eram vítimas de desigualdades, por exemplo as pessoas negras; era uma coisa que sempre me afetou."

and returning home also in the dark, in the evenings, when her mother finished working.

Tereza aimed to study social services, but she was not able to pursue a place in a public university as the course was unavailable in her home town. She could not afford the living costs outside her parent's home or studying full-time as she needed to work during the day. Her mother told me that Tereza received a low-quality public secondary education. She struggled to pass the exams to enter university, spending two years preparing herself for it after failing at her first attempt. On Saturdays she studied at EDUCAFRO[78], an NGO that provides free preparatory courses to enter university to black and low-income individuals, and on weekdays she attended a paid preparatory course after being granted a scholarship to study in the evenings. The scholarship required that she worked in an unpaid internship during the day. During this period her parents "didn't count on my wages at home"[79], she recalls, as she was busy working during the day, and studying during the evenings and on Saturdays.

Tereza was offered a place at her second attempt to enter university. The offer was from the Pontifical Catholic University of São Paulo (PUC-SP), a private, non-profit university. She told me there were no funding programmes and affirmative action policies when she started university in 2002. She took a bank loan to pay for her matriculation fee and despite being granted a scholarship for her studies, she still had to pay back 50% of the course tuition fees after completing it (she settled her student debt in 2020). She had little time for her studies as she worked full-time in a paid job during the day while studying in the evenings at university. She also worked at her family's food stall on Sundays.

Although her parents were not able to help her financially to pay for her university fees, Tereza says that they did all they could to keep their children at school when they were young: "we were able to take our time [her brother and herself] … before having to get a paid job"[80], she says. She told me that she and her brother were lucky, compared to other relatives of the same generation that started working when they were thirteen or fourteen years old. "My parents helped us as much as they could when we were young [to

---

[78] https://www.educafro.org.br
[79] "não contaram com a minha renda de trabalho em casa."
[80] "nós demoramos para trabalhar aqui em casa."

save us having to get a paid job] so we could prioritize our studies"[81], she adds. Due to that, she was able to finish her education without having to have a paid job until she started university.

Tereza dreamed of an academic degree, but most people suggested otherwise: *"you need a professional degree [as opposed to a university one], you have to become a teacher!"*[82]. She recalls other people telling her this often, advising her to choose a programme that would lead her to entry-to-practice professions so she would have a job quicker. She remembers that her mother always challenged these people, telling them: "my daughter can be whatever she wants to be!"[83], she recalls.

Tereza told me that both her parents prioritized their children's education and were present in their school life. They did what they could to give them the means to study as well as the encouragement to pursue it:

My parents always nurtured the culture of study at our home – they've always put our education first: a place to study at home ... and I was always gifted with many books; my parents were always present in my school life, and they always told me that it was possible that I could go to university[84]. (Tereza)

Tereza also counted on a very supportive community around her: she was gifted books by black women who were teachers living in her neighbourhood, received support from people from the black movement and teachers from EDUCAFRO. She was the only daughter I interviewed who also counted on the support from her community and NGOs. That additional support was crucial for her to thrive in her educational journey.

Tereza's story portrays the challenges faced by young, poor, black women in Brazil, showing how this group of minoritized girls is highly affected by multiple inequalities. This was sharply exposed during the 2020 global pandemic when educational conditions in Brazil – and in many other

---

[81] "Meus pais seguraram o máximo para que a gente pudesse priorizar os estudos."
[82] "tem que fazer ensino técnico, ser professora!"
[83] "minha filha pode ser o que ela quiser!"
[84] "Em casa sempre teve uma cultura do estudo, meus pais sempre colocaram como uma prioridade: um lugar para estudar ... eu sempre ganhei muitos livros, meus pais sempre foram muito presentes na escola, e sempre disseram pra mim que seria possível entrar numa universidade".

places – were worsened, exposing gender, racial and social disparities, among others. The study *Education of Black Girls in Times of the Pandemic: Deepening Inequalities* (Geledés, 2021) analysed the impact of the pandemic on the lives of children attending state-funded schools in São Paulo. It was found that black families were affected more than white families as the only educational model available during the school closures was remote learning. Black families lacked computer resources at home as well as access to the internet in comparison to white families. The study also shows that black girls were more affected by the lack of study material at home in comparison to white girls and black boys.

Tereza is likely to be an exception in comparison to other black women in the country – a black woman who achieved educational qualifications further than most of her peers. Of all the daughters I interviewed, Tereza is the one with the higher level of formal education among them and the only black woman. After her struggle to enter and finish university in a private institution, she was offered a place in the master's programme of the University of São Paulo, the same top public university where Lucia did her undergraduate studies. After finishing her master's, she published an academic book in Brazil based on her research about state violence against black people in poor communities in São Paulo. Then, she started her PhD in architecture in the same institution. She was on maternity leave from her PhD at the time we had our conversations, taking care of her newborn daughter, Carolina.

2.3 Paula

Paula told me that her mother worked long hours during her childhood, including Saturdays, and that she was raised by her grandparents from six to fifteen years old – her mother corrected that later and told me that she moved back with her when she was thirteen, not fifteen. Paula accompanied her mother to work many times before moving with her grandparents, when she was little. "The most remarkable memory I have [from her childhood] is of us [her mother and herself] using public transport in the morning, crowded with people, and my mother carrying me in her arms along with many other things she had to carry. It was a real struggle"[85], she recalls. She resents her mother not being able to be more present and wished Val could have spent more time with her during her childhood, to play and to be around her.

Paula told me that she would never have a university degree without support from her mother and her mother's employer. She studied social communication and journalism at Paulista University (UNIP), a private, for-profit institution. She lived with Val while preparing to pass the university's entrance test, and during university. She worked from home during the pandemic and has a position as an analyst. She achieved financial independence through her job and has a comfortable life that allows her to study other languages and travel abroad, and she completed a self-funded post-graduate course.

2.4 Helena

Helena told me that she is the first and the only person in her close family group to go to university. She had more opportunities than her mother did: "My mother didn't have the opportunity to go to university. She didn't even finish school, she had to leave when she was in the fifth year"[86]. She adds that Vitória lived in a very different context from hers: "Also because she [Vitória] was born in a place deprived of ... everything ... anything, in the backlands of the northeast. She got married early, right, she was a mother early. Then, when she migrated to São Paulo, there was no time, right, to pursue and finish school. [She] had to work to maintain herself"[87].

Helena told me that her mother Vitória was absent during her childhood and teenage years. The family lived in the periphery of Campinas and that consumed more hours from her mother's busy life as they relied on the

---

[85] "A lembrança que mais tenho é do transporte público pela manhã, lotado de pessoas e minha mãe me carregando com muitas coisas. Fazendo um grande esforço."
[86] "Minha mãe não teve oportunidade de fazer faculdade. Ela nem terminou os estudos, ela precisou parar no quinto ano."
[87] "Até porque ela nasceu num lugar muito desprovido de ... tudo ... de qualquer coisa, no sertão do nordeste. Ela se casou cedo, né, foi mãe cedo. Aí, quando veio pra são Paulo, não tinha muito tempo, né, pra ir procurar e terminar os estudos. Precisava trabalhar pra se sustentar."

precarious public transport to move around the city. Helena is the youngest of the daughters I interviewed, and her mother was able to count on the free state-funded day care available from Helena's early years, allowing her to work full-time. Vitória did the school trips before and after work; she worked on weekdays and Saturdays. Her family only had Sundays together – but then the mother was busy cleaning and organizing their own home, according to Helena.

When asked about what she would do for her child that her mother did not do for her, Helena told me that she would create a reading culture at home:

> *I think I would be more resilient encouraging [my child's] studies, however, I know that my mother didn't do it for me because nobody did it for her', right ... also [I would] incentivise reading, things that she didn't have [Vitória]. It was not from her culture, but now as an adult, I suffer a lot because I find it difficult to read a book. Now that I am old, I am trying to create the habit, I am reading more, but I didn't do it before, right. So, to me, it was hard to sit down and study for the exams when I was at school, it was always very complicated because I didn't have the routine of reading when I was little, and I believe I would start doing that to my child*[88]. (Helena)

Helena is aware of the educational deprivation experienced by her mother and how that affected Vitória's capacity of reading to her when she was little. She is also conscious about how this became a vicious cycle that crosses generations, having a negative impact on herself. She wants to break this cycle with her child. Her testimonial is at the core of social mobility; being aware of the oppressive forces experienced by her mother and herself, she can actively build on her way out, on her own social mobility, planning to pass it forward and further to her child.

---

[88] "Eu acho que eu seria mais insistente em relação aos estudos, porém eu sei que a minha mãe não fez isso porque não fizeram isso com ela, né ... e incentivo a leitura, coisas que ela não teve. Não foi da cultura dela, mas hoje eu sofro muito pra conseguir ler um livro. Agora, depois de velha, eu tô tentando criar o hábito, eu tô lendo mais, só que eu não fazia isso, né. Então, pra mim, na escola, sentar pra estudar pra provas e tal, sempre foi muito complicado, porque eu não tinha o hábito de ler desde pequena e eu acho que eu faria isso pela minha filha."

Helena stopped studying and moved out of her parents' home to live with her boyfriend when she was sixteen years old. She had to catch up with her secondary school studies later: "[…] I left school when I was sixteen years, I moved in with my boyfriend at the time, and that slowed me down in a way, right. Later I had to catch up with my studies before going to university"[89].

She told me she wanted to be a teacher and worked with children for the year before starting university to confirm her vocation. She has a degree in education from the Paulista University (UNIP), the same private, for-profit institution where Paula obtained her degree. Helena told me that she did not have to study hard to pass the university's exams: "the entrance exams [to enter university] were not very challenging because I did not apply for a place at a federal university, I applied for a place in a private one so I believe that their [acceptance] criteria is not that, you know, that strict"[90].

Helena said that, differently from some of her friends, she did not apply for government funding programmes such as FIES or ProUni: "I preferred to make an effort and work to pay for it"[91], she says. Helena told me that she paid her university tuition fees. Her mother, however, claims to have paid for it herself: "If it was up to Helena to work and pay for her studies, she would have never had her university degree […] I had to give up some of my own money to pay for her university fees … I didn't take a loan, the money came from my own wages!"[92] Vitória also told me that she worked overtime, Saturdays, and sometimes gave up of part of her holidays to gather additional funds to support her family.

Helena is the only daughter I interviewed that did not achieve financial stability after obtaining a degree, possibly due to a combination of career choice with a degree from a low-quality higher education institution. Her

---

[89] "[...] eu larguei os estudos aos dezesseis anos, fui morar com um namorado na época e isso de uma forma me atrasou um pouco, né. Depois fui fazê supletivo pra pode entrá na faculdade."
[90] "O vestibular não foi algo que eu precisei estudar muito porque como eu não prestei uma universidade federal, foi uma universidade particular, eu acredito que eles não avaliam assim, sabe, super de maneira assídua."
[91] "eu preferi me esforçar mesmo e trabalhar e pagar."
[92] "se a Helena fosse depender dela pra pagar a faculdade, ela não teria feito a faculdade [...] eu tive que abrir mão de um dinheiro meu … não fiz empréstimo, foi do meu salário mesmo!"

own experience made her very sceptical about higher education: "I believe that, nowadays, a degree won't help you achieve all that you want to achieve. Of course it will help you to stand out but, nowadays, a degree doesn't have the same weight it had in the old days."[93]. The "old days" she is referring to is before what some call the start of the mercantilization of higher education in the country that started in 1997, when for-profit institutions were regulated by law, differing themselves from other private, non-profit institutions and expanding their presence (Carvalho, 2013).

Despite struggling with her finances after securing a job linked to her degree, Helena achieved a higher social status compared to her mother, as a primary school teacher. Helena said that her mother was unhappy with her choice of course as teachers are undervalued and badly paid in Brazil, but Vitória supported her, nonetheless. She did not mention her mother's financial aid in our conversation.

Helena had a baby in the beginning of 2021. She was on maternity leave from her teaching job when we had our conversations. After that, she adopted a child from a relative who died. I met Helena, her partner and children in person when I visited Brazil in 2022. She told me she was back to work after her maternity leave and working full-time to raise her children who are in full-time nursery and school. Since having the children, she moved close to her mother and now they can spend more time together.

2.5 Julia

Julia is Carmem's daughter. She is the only daughter I have interviewed that had to start working early, when she was fourteen years old. She worked at McDonalds and was able to reconcile job and studies, but not without difficulties. When she started university, almost all her wages were used to pay her university tuition fees. Like Paula and Helena, she was offered a place at Paulista University (UNIP) a private, for-profit institution. She studied beauty in the evenings and worked during the day, and she lived with her family, avoiding additional living costs. She mentioned that her family always helped her emotionally and they also supported her

---

[93] "Mas eu acredito que, hoje em dia, não é um diploma que vai te fazê conquistá tudo o que você qué. Claro que é um diferencial, mas hoje em dia o diploma não vale tanto quanto valia antigamente."

financially at times when she struggled to pay her tuition fees. She is the only daughter I interviewed that has a professional degree rather than an academic one.

She currently works as shop assistant in a women's clothes store in Campinas and has a child with her husband. She has achieved a better social status and income, compared to her mother, and told me that she was able to purchase her own home – something not achieved by Carmem yet – when she was twenty-eight years old. However, I have no information to help me understand further if the comfortable life she has was possible because of her job, or her husband's – or, most likely, both.

2.6 Findings

All daughters of domestic workers received high levels of support from their mothers, according to their own circumstances. Marilla was able to pay for her daughter to attend a preparatory course to enter university and that gave her an advantage, compared to the other women I interviewed, as Lucia was the only one to be offered a place in a top, public university. She was also the only one achieving some level of financial autonomy after leaving her parent's house while at university, and was able to finance her living costs with the internship opportunities offered by her university while also working as an English teacher. The other daughters went to private universities, one to a non-profit institution and the others to the same for-profit institution (at different times and on different courses). Tereza was offered a place at a non-profit university, but it took her two years to prepare herself for the exams; she attended a private preparatory course in the evenings on weekdays (paid for with her internship work at the school during the day) combined with a free course offered by an NGO on Saturdays. Helena, Paula and Julia did not attend a preparatory course and were all offered a place at a for-profit university. The fact that they went to private institutions brought an additional layer of pressure on themselves and their families: tuition fees were high, and many did not have the option of studying full-time, as they needed to work during the day. Also, they all lived with their parents and their education was restricted to the same city they lived in, as they could not afford living costs outside their parents' home. This also determined the options they had for the course of study and at least one of the daughters, Tereza, was only able to pursue the programme she wanted at the cost of attending a private institution because it was not available at the public one in her city. It took her almost twenty years to settle her student debt. Val and Vitória were able to pay their daughters' tuition fees; Val with her employer's help, Vitória with the additional income earned by working more hours including overtime, giving up some days of annual leave in exchange for extra pay and working on Saturdays. All mothers supported their daughters by providing food, study materials and helping with transport costs related to their studies at the cost of working even longer hours, not spending their money on themselves and compromising their presence at home as they had to work more to afford it all.

Despite their mother's support, all daughters had to work while at university – some to afford tuition fees, others to cover their living costs. Some daughters had no financial support from their fathers whatsoever and could only rely on their mothers and themselves. Only Tereza benefited from scholarship programmes – a partial one, offered by her university, not through the government's programmes. She is the only one that also received support outside her family, from organizations such as EDUCAFRO and her community.

Most daughters experienced intergenerational social mobility in both income and social status after obtaining a university degree. Their mother's commitment to their education allowed them to go beyond university and enter other social spaces through internships and social networks that eventually led them to employment, like Lucia and Paula. Education, notably higher education, was a priority within their families as they believed a degree would bring better life opportunities. Even if mothers were not able to support their daughters financially, they helped them in other important ways, like Dandara did, by removing the pressure on Tereza to work at an early age and by empowering her to fight racism and be confident about herself. Julia, however, had to work when she was still a teenager but counted on her family's supportive environment nevertheless and kept herself at school while living with her parents. All stories highlight the fragility of these women's trajectories, even when receiving such levels of support.

All the daughters I have interviewed acknowledged the importance of their mother's role in their pursuit of education and showed a strong desire to compensate them for their sacrifices, and to help their mothers to overcome their challenging life conditions. They carry a "genetic pain" from their mothers that can now be attenuated or repaired as the younger generation has achieved better income and social status. Daughters are now able to provide for their mothers emotionally – if not able to also help them materially – overcoming their traumas altogether. This is the topic of the next chapter.

Chapter Three

Intertwined Memories (Mothers and Daughters)

"I never cared, only about myself"[94] (Lucia)

Hirsch's postmemory phenomenon is often present in the narratives of the daughters of domestic workers I interviewed, highly connected to acute poverty experienced by their mothers. That left these women without many life choices and required them to cope with traumatic pain such as separating themselves from their children. However, the dynamics of this memory transmission is not straightforward as the memories of mothers and daughters were highly intertwined. While some traumatic stories were orally passed from domestic workers to their daughters, other memories were shared between mothers and daughters as they lived them together.

I have observed in my interviews that the mother's traumatic memories are counterbalanced by the satisfaction experienced later in life, derived from the life achievements of their daughters, at both personal and professional levels. The mothers live their daughter's positive experiences as if they were their own, carrying these happy memories forward in their lives. The fact that their daughters have escaped the fate of being domestic workers resonates deeply with their mothers: their daughter's victory is their own victory. Like the "genetic pain" transmitted from mothers to their daughters, achievements are also shared between the two generations of women, passed from daughters to mothers when vicious cycles are broken. I call these complex dynamics of memory transmission "intertwined memories". Built upon the postmemory theory in which the generation after bears the traumatic experiences of those who came before, my theory of intertwined memory shows that memories also travel the other way around,

---

[94] "Nunca pensei só em mim."

from the younger generation back to the previous one. Similar to the mechanism of transmission of traumatic memories, the outstanding positive ones experienced when the younger generation breaks cycles of inequality and poverty bounce back to their mothers. Happy memories linked to moments when these women broke intergenerational vicious cycles that caused trauma in the first place are the positive correspondent of the postmemory. While the postmemory is a one-way transmission of memory, the intertwined memory theory shows that intergenerational memory has a two-way dynamic of transmission. Mothers' and daughters' memories related to individual trauma as well as the ones built upon great achievements are transmitted and shared between these women in an intertwined manner, affecting their lives and identities.

The life stories of mothers and daughters I interviewed showed that experiences of social mobility after the first-generation university entrants obtained a degree had a material dimension, but also a correlated process was observed at the level of their emotions and mental health. Intergenerational inequalities and experiences of poverty limited their mothers' and grandmothers' access to higher education and to more dignified working conditions, feeding vicious cycles of poor mental health among these women that were hard to break.

I argue that the intertwined memories of these women triggered a great amount of effort from the daughters I interviewed to repair their mothers, helping in the healing process of their mothers' emotional scars and with their own once they had achieved a better social status and income, strengthening social mobility of this first generation of women that went to university.

3.1 Marilla and Lucia

Lucia started our conversation by telling me about her mother and her family's history. I learned more about Marilla's life when interviewing Lucia than through the conversation I had with Marilla herself. She shared with me a little of her mother's history:

My mother, she is the daughter of Japanese [parents], but her story is a little different from the other Japanese immigrants that came to Brazil, who brought their families and all, right ... my grandfather, he came alone ...

when he was fourteen ... he worked with agriculture, right. ... My mother comes from a poor family. ... My mother grew in a small farm and her sisters and herself, except, I think, for the youngest one, had to start life working as maids. My mother started – she says – working at her teacher's house, like, looking after her child, my own mother being very young. At that time, my mother had studied up to the fourth year, only later that she caught up with her studies, while I was at primary school; she did primary education when adult. She had forty something, forty-five, I think ... well ... she only studied until the fourth year, then she worked as a maid for a long time, working at other family's house, she used to say; first [she worked] in the farm, [then] as maid; then she got a job as receptionist in Sao Paulo. She comes from a family of nine siblings ... and from my father's side they were eight siblings, so they came from those big families, right. Because of that, my mother and my father are those type of people who tried to better their lives by leaving their local area. ... After they got married, because they had children, my mother had to stop working and they had five children; they kept having children, kept having children and [my father] jumped from one job to the other. My father didn't have drinking problems or anything like that, he was just uncapable of keeping a job. And then, when my mother was on her third child, if I am not mistaken – and by that time she was back to work as a maid, sometimes on Saturdays – and later she managed to work as a school cleaner in a state-funded school, what she did for twenty-five years, like, of her life ... and then, on her last ten years of work she worked also as a cleaner in a Court of Justice[95]. (Lucia)

---

[95] "A minha mãe, ela é filha de japoneses, mas a história dela é um pouco diferente dos japoneses que normalmente vieram ao Brasil, que vieram com família e tal, né ... o meu avô, ele veio sozinho ... aos quatorze anos ... ele trabalhava com agricultura, né. ... Minha mãe vem de uma família pobre ... Minha mãe veio da roça e ela e as irmãs praticamente todas, tirando, acho, que a mais nova, tiveram que começar a vida trabalhando de doméstica. A minha mãe começou – ela fala até - que ela tava na casa da professora dela, assim, cuidava do filho, ela lá, novinha. Minha mãe, na época tinha feito só até o quarto ano, depois é que ela fez um supletivo, enquanto eu fazia meu fundamental, ela fez o fundamental no supletivo. Ela já tava com 40 e poucos anos, 45 anos, acho ... Aí ela só estudou até o quarto [ano], daí ficou trabalhando de doméstica por bastante tempo, assim, em casa de família, né, que ela falava; primeiro na roça, casa de família; e depois ela conseguiu um emprego de recepcionista em São Paulo. Ela vem de uma família de nove irmãos ... e do meu pai oito irmãos, então aquelas famílias numerosas, né. Então tanto ela como meu pai são aquelas pessoas, né, que tentavam melhorar de vida saindo da sua região local, assim ... Depois que eles casaram, por causa de filho, a minha mãe parou de trabalhar e meu pai depois teve cinco filhos; foi tendo filhos, foi tendo filhos, e ai pulava de um

When I asked Lucia about her childhood memories, she told me that they are marked by experiences of deprivation and her mother's struggle to raise herself and her four siblings. She told me her family never had holiday trips together due to the lack of money and that one of the "unusual" things she really wished as a child was to have her clothes washed with fabric softener, a smell she loved. At that time, she says, luxury to her was to wear clothes that smelled of fabric softener but the product was too expensive, and her family could not afford it.

She recalls that her mother often told the children "I wish I could jump on a train and run away from here"[96] as Marilla could not cope with the family's difficulties. She told me that these memories are so painful that she decided not to be a mother herself: "I experienced many traumas [because of her family] … to me, having a family wasn't something to be pursued"[97], she says.

The mother was also aggressive: "she would hit anything that crossed her path"[98], says Lucia. She recalls an occasion when she was five years old, and she and her brother were accompanying their mother to work. She accidentally broke a mirror from the school where their mother worked as cleaner and Marilla was enraged: she took the children to a dark room, removed their clothes and spanked them, leaving them crying alone in the room. The head teacher at the school was merciless and made Marilla pay for the broken mirror in several instalments. This episode marked Lucia: "I was highly traumatized at the time … I've already worked on that in my psychotherapy sessions"[99], she says, and tells me that the school's head teacher was so difficult that she still remembers his full name.

---

emprego pro outro. Meu pai não tinha problema de bebida nada, mas ele não conseguia se manter fixo em emprego. E aí quando minha mãe tava no terceiro filho, se não me engano, aí ela – nisso ela já tava trabalhando numas casas de família, às vezes de sábado – e depois ela conseguiu trabalhar de servente de escola, numa escola do estado, que é o que ela fez durante vinte e cinco anos, assim, da vida ... e depois nos últimos 10 anos de vida servente também, assim, de faxineira, num tribunal."

[96] "queria pegar um trem e fugir."
[97] "eu tive muito trauma ... pra mim família não parecia ser um valor máximo."
[98] "tudo o que ela achava na frente ela batia."
[99] "eu fiquei com muito trauma na época, eu já trabalhei isso na terapia."

Lucia also recalls accompanying her mother to the dentist when she was an infant and being traumatized by seeing the dentist using a dirty piece of cloth to clean her mother's mouth while extracting her teeth. Marilla could not afford a good dentist and ended up in the hands of a professional with poor hygiene – and possibly poor skills. She lost all of her teeth and Lucia recalls her mother saying "look what life has gifted me"[100], every time Marilla took the prosthetic teeth out. One of Lucia's main concerns when she was younger was to have a job that allowed her to have good dental and medical care for herself and her mother: "I never cared only about myself because I could see my family's struggles"[101], she says, adding that "I would feel very bad if my mother died because I couldn't afford to pay for her medical treatment"[102].

Lucia told me that Marilla constantly told her children: "you have to study so you can be a person better than me"[103]. When I asked Lucia if becoming a civil servant was her mother's idea, she adamantly denied it, despite initially telling me about the pressure her mother put on her to become a civil servant. Lucia told me that other people around her had pursued the same path as aiming at a civil service career in Brazil is rather a widespread idea among people seeking a stable job, not an idea that only her mother had.

Despite Lucia's resentment and apparent distance from her mother, she has a strong desire to help her: "I am very happy that I was able to help my mother as I wanted"[104], she says. Due to Lucia's stable career, she is now able to have a private health plan for herself and to offer one to Marilla. She recalls that her mother has already benefited from it, avoiding having an unnecessary operation indicated by a doctor in the public national health system after getting a second opinion from a private one. She also gifted her parents with a fridge and paid for family holidays together, including the expenses of her brother with special needs.

---

[100] "olha só o que eu ganhei nessa vida..
[101] "Nunca pensei só em mim, porque eu via as dificuldades da família."
[102] "eu vou ficar muito mal se minha mãe morrer porque eu não tinha dinheiro para poder pagar um tratamento médico."
[103] 'você tem que estudar, pra você ser alguém melhor do que eu fui'.
[104] "sou muito feliz de já conseguir ter feito o que eu queria pela minha mãe."

She wishes to help Marilla further on an emotional level as well and she told me that she had the opportunity to do that during the global pandemic. She recalls that she was able to bring joy to her mother, by giving her books to read as well as bringing her DVDs to watch when she was isolating during the pandemic. Lucia says her mother never had time for herself and the gifts helped Marilla to escape from her reality. For the first time, she says, she saw her mother less worried and nurturing dreams. Lucia remembers she was visiting her parents one day and could not find Marilla in the kitchen after lunch – the place she would always be, cleaning the dishes. Instead, she spotted her mother reading in her backyard. "I had forgotten how romantic I am"[105], Lucia recalls her mother saying after reading Jane Austen's novels and L. M. Montgomery's *Anne of Green Gables*. She thinks her mother is less bitter now at an older age, and Lucia told me in a very lyrical way that Marilla recently told her that she is finally "seeing life" and she is grateful for the life she has.

3.2 Dandara and Tereza

Dandara showed joy in the conversations we had about her daughter Tereza. Talking about her daughter makes her feel good. She said:

It is a pleasure to have this opportunity to talk about my daughter. My daughter is a source of pride, you know Anna, right. Like ... she did, right, social service, right, at PUC, right, I am saying, right. She did her doctorate at USP and she finished, right, her master's ... at USP, right. And there was something else: the book was born, right ... a book was born: [she attempts to say the long title of Tereza's first academic published book], right. So, to me, it is a great source of pride, right, because ... why am I telling you this? That she is a source of pride to me? My grandmother, right, she couldn't read and write. My mother could neither, right. My mother also couldn't read but they, my ancestors, they had something [in common]: [they had] a strong wisdom, right. Indeed. [They were] faith healers, midwives, right ... [they did] those things, always helping others and [they] always said,

---

[105] "Eu não lembrava que eu era tão romântica assim."

including my mother: 'never keep your eyes down! Go ahead, fight, right'[106]. (Dandara)

Tereza is currently doing her PhD in one of the most prestigious public universities in Brazil (USP). She is a mature student around her forties. When I spoke to her, she was on maternity leave. Her daughter Carolina was born while she was doing her doctorate studies during the first year of the global pandemic in 2020. Like her mother, she mentioned that she carries her family's black *ancestry* with her (the word used by mother and daughter is imbued with a spiritual force) and recalls her family's history. She told me that Dandara had finished primary education when adult and both her grandmothers were unable to read and write, one catching up with primary education when she was sixty-five years old. Her mother also recalls a little of her heritage, giving me more details about the racialized identities of the women in her family:

I had very little education, I had indeed, very little education. What do I mean? I ... my parents struggled to raise us, right. We were twelve siblings, but, despite that, my mother said: 'children: you have to study! Study! Study! Black people, right – she said it like this – we, black people ... it is so difficult ... the fight is so difficult ...' Why? Because my mother's grandmother was a slave, she was a slave, right. So, I did the same [as her mother]: with my little education, I always empowered my daughter, my children, my siblings, you understand? I decided, I said: 'look, people, you don't have to be a doctor, but you have to have a degree'. In the old days it was called 'a degree', right. You have to have a degree, to be proud of what you do. Don't be ashamed! Go forward[107]. (Dandara)

---

[106] "É um prazer essa oportunidade de falar sobre minha filha. A minha filha é um orgulho pra mim, sabe Anna, né. Que nem ... ela fez, né, serviço social, né, na PUC, né, falando, né. Fez o doutorado da USP e depois terminou, né, o mestrado ... na USP, né. E teve uma grande também: nasceu o livro, né ... nasce um livro: [tentativa de falar o título do livro], né. Então, pra mim é muito orgulho, né, porque ... porque que eu falo isso pra você? Que é orgulho? A minha avó, né, não sabia ler e nem escrever. Minha mãe também não, né. Minha mãe também não sabia ler, mas elas, a ancestralidade, tinham uma coisa: a sabedoria muito forte, né. Sim Benzedeira, parteira, né ... essas coisas de ajudar sempre o próximo e sempre falá, inclusive minha mãe: "nunca abaixe esse olhar! Vai em frente, vai na luta, né."
[107] "E eu tive um pouco estudo, eu tive sim um pouco estudo. Como assim? Eu... muita dificuldade teve meus pais pra criar nóis (né?) Nós era em 12 irmãos, mas

Racism and discrimination were present in Tereza's life from the early days, but she was silent about it in our conversations – I learned about it from her mother. Dandara said: "[Tereza] was always conscious [about her positionality]: 'I am a girl, black, so I have to fight to achieve my objectives'. I truly admire that. That already comes ... say ... from within herself, understand … it comes from within herself"[108].

The mother told me that when Tereza was a child she struggled with the bully she suffered at school because of her afro hair. Dandara recalls:

I know that there is prejudice against her colour [Tereza's], right. Because she was very criticized [Dandara laughs out loud], they called her names, understand? So, I said that: 'oh, heavenly God, it is going to be now, right'. And about the hair [her daughter's afro hair] – what I recall – is that I was braiding her hair, right. I did many braids ... and the others made fun of her, right, you know how children are. So ... the prejudice is like this: it is there, it exists, but children don't see it, right. What is the meaning of it? What is going on? They watch adults speaking [racist abuse]. So I told her [Tereza]: 'my daughter, we are black – thanks to God. You will hear many things, many things. It might not be now that you are hearing that [racist abuse] ... but I want you to study, to raise your head, to fight. Where ... you go wherever you want to go, right! You go. Don't be ashamed, don't be ashamed of being black. Don't be ashamed of having a hair, right ... a hair like ... like your hair! Don't be ashamed of your hair because we are black and that is how it is, right'[109]. (Dandara)

---

mesmo assim a minha mãe falava: "gente: estuda! Estuda, estuda! Gente preto (né?) – ela falava desse jeito – nóis, preto ... é tão difícil... a luta é tão difícil..." Porque? Porque a avó da minha mãe era escrava, foi escrava (né?) Então pra mim também, com meu pouco estudo, eu sempre fortaleci a minha filha, os meus filhos, os meus sobrinhos, entendeu? Tracei, falei: "olha gente, não precisa ser doutor, mas tem que ter um diproma". Antigamente era o diploma (né?). Você tem que ter o diploma, tem que ter orgulho que você faz. Não tenha vergonha! Vai em frente."

[108] "[Tereza] sempre teve aquela consciência: "eu sô uma menina, negra, então eu tenho que lutá pra consegui o meu objetivo". Eu admiro muito. Isso já vem ... assim ... dela mesmo, entendeu ... já vem dela mesmo".

[109] 'Eu sei que tem aquele preconceito de cor, né. Porque ela foi muito criticada [ela ri alto], xingava ela, entendeu? Então eu falei assim: "meu deus do céu, vai ser agora, né". E sobre o cabelo – que eu lembro – que eu tava trançando o cabelo dela, né. O que eu fazia que era bastante trancinha ... e os pessoal caçoava, né, sabe como criança é. Então ... o preconceito é assim: existe e tem, mas criança não sabia, né. O que era

When Dandara says that children reproduce racism after seeing adults being racist without realizing what they are doing, she is pointing out to what Sriprakash et al. describe as learning whiteness (2022) when systems of white domination that are not natural to a child, or anyone, are forged and kept though practices of colonial violence and racial injustice. According to Liz Pemberton (Anna Freud Centre, 2022), who specializes in racial trauma and anti-racist training in the early years sector in the UK, discussions about race and racial trauma at schools in the early years are often avoided and are not a priority. She says there is a pushback arguing that children are too young to talk about racism or to experience it. Talking about this subject is commonly seem as harmful, as an interruption in their "idyllic" childhood. Pemberton then asks: "whose idyllic childhood? whose childhood are we talking about actually?" Peter (Anna Freud Centre, 2022) adds that not talking about those subjects does not make the problem go away, they just go underground and later come out in the form of behaviour. In children, it comes out in their entire development of self – both in children that are likely to be victims of racism and children that are more likely to hold racist ideas without necessarily being aware of them.

Advocating for prioritizing anti-racist conversations at schools in the UK, Pemberton (Anna Freud Centre, 2022) argues that children at three years old are already exploring complex concepts and schools in the country have campaigns to teach children at this age about having agency over their bodies, for example, with the purpose to keep children safe from sexual abuse. The sensitive topic is labelled under the "safeguarding umbrella", she says, as it is highly important that children understand that. Racism and racial trauma, on the other hand, are often labelled under the "dangerous umbrella". That is a mistake, she argues, as those important conversations introduce topics around justice and children have an acute awareness of fairness. Pemberton points out that children will always tell "what is fair"

---

dizê isto aí? O que acontecia? Via o adulto falar, não é mesmo? Então eu peguei, eu falei pra ela: "minha filha, nós somos negros - graças a deus. Você vai escutar muitas, muitas coisa. Não é agora que você está escutando isto aí... mas eu quero que você estude, cabeça erguida, vai na sua luta. Aonde ... Você entra aonde você quisé, né! Você entra. Não tenha vergonha, não tenha vergonha de ser negra. Não tenha vergonha de ter o cabelo, né ... o cabelo mais ... o cabelo seu! Não tenha vergonha do seu cabelo porque a gente é negra e é assim mesmo, né?"

and "what is not fair" and "why they think it is fair" or "not fair", arguing that they can understand conversations about justice, equity and fairness.

While Dandara chose to share Tereza's childhood memories of suffering racism, Tereza decided to share the other side of these memories by telling me about her mother's role giving her love and caring for her hair, helping her to build self-love. This shaped her childhood, helping her to build a positive sense of self, which, according to Liz Pemberton, is particularly important for the well-being and mental wellness of racially minoritized[110] children since, as pointed out by Sarah Peter, these children often find mental health services hard to reach (Anna Freud Centre, 2022).

Tereza told me about Dandara's daily ritual of braiding her hair in the evenings, after long hours at work: "when she [Dandara] arrived home, she still found time to do plaits in my hair"[111], she recalls. Valuing and being proud of their black phenotypes are key to the validation of black women's power (Berth, 2019). Tereza told me that she grew up a confident woman as a result of the loving and caring environment at home. The routine of love and care also touched Tereza's learning experience, as she recalls:

Despite working a lot, my mother gave me a lot of support. I remember that she [Dandara] arrived home tired from work and helped me with my school homework, helped me to decorate my schoolbooks, made sure I had finished all my schoolwork. We [herself and her brother] started year one [at school] already knowing how to read and write and this is highly related to the kind of support we had at home. They [parents] did a lot, a lot indeed and I am very grateful to that and that is a source of inspiration for myself[112]. (Tereza)

---

[110] Liz Pemberton (Anna Freud, 2022) highlights that using words with intention is very important when working with anti-racist practices. She argues that black and brown children and their families are minoritized being part of the global majority. She used the term "racially minoritized" children to highlight Rosemary Campbell Stephens' (2021) work that reclaims the term "global majority" by a majority that has been racialised as "ethnic minorities" as a form of neo-colonialism.
[111] "quando chegava em casa, ela [Dandara] ainda trançava o meu cabelo."
[112] "Mesmo trabalhando tanto a minha mãe me deu muito suporte. Eu lembro que ela [Dandara] chegava cansada do trabalho e me ajudava com dever de escola, ajudava a cuidar do caderno, via se eu tinha feito a lição. A gente entrou, assim, na primeira série já sabendo assim ler e escrever e isso tem muita relação com o acompanhamento que a gente tinha em casa. Então, dentro das limitações, eles fizeram muito, muito mesmo e eu sou muito grata e me inspiro muito."

The day-to-day care is essential for a child to develop a healthy self-esteem and that will make them become confident of their own human value, their capacity to love and care for others (Goldstein et al., 1980b). Tereza is a mature woman now and had her first child recently. She wishes to repeat what her mother did to her with her daughter.

The mother had an important role in Tereza's process of self-definition, helping her to craft her own identity, especially important for black women to challenge the stereotypical images of themselves created by the intersecting oppressions of classism, racism and sexism that they experience (Collins, 2000).

Tereza has plenty of memories linked to the empowerment received from her mother:

> *She [Dandara] always found a way to be present at the school's meetings, celebrations and events, and to clap for me and to tell me that I looked beautiful [...] she was always a voice saying that things were possible for me*[113]. (Tereza)

Despite all the empowerment received, Tereza was not confident to start university, scared of this environment so distant from her reality. As noted by Berth (2019), empowering black women is an important step to the construction of self-love but it is also necessary that black people occupy spaces of power in society, to have representativity and redefine imaginaries. For that, Tereza gave her own contribution, paving the way for other black women, occupying a space at university, followed by a successful academic career at an elite institution. She recalls that she was encouraged by a teacher that told her: "Tereza, do you know who are you bringing to university with you? You are bringing your father, your mother, the history of your family, your experiences from the samba school and from the black movement ..."[114].

---

[112] "Nas reuniões da escola, nas festinhas, nos eventos, ela [Dandara] dava um jeito de aparecer, de bater palma, de falar que eu tava bonita [...] sempre foi uma voz dizendo que era possível."
[114] "Tereza, sabe quem você vai levar para a universidade? Você vai levar o seu pai, a sua mãe, a história da sua família, suas vivências na escola de samba, no movimento negro …".

Tereza figuratively took her mother and the special people in her life to university with her: "It was a good way of arriving, [at university] carrying this special rucksack filled with these special people"[115], she says.

Dandara says that one of the best days of her life was when her daughter invited her to her matriculation ceremony when she was offered a place at the master's programme at USP. She told me:

> *I get very emotional, right, when we talk about it ... This was ... this is! ... my biggest dream. My biggest dream [coming true]. That is how I see it: all that I was unable to have, my children have now, right. Such as: I was very proud that she [Tereza] asked me, right, before her matriculation ceremony at USP ... she came to me and said: 'mother, would you like to come with me for my matriculation ceremony?' [Tereza invited] the parents, right, myself and my husband. I said to her: 'Tereza ... my daughter ... what a [wonderful] present you are giving me'. You [Anna] have no idea how proud I was to see her signing her matriculation there at USP. There, where ... I told her [Tereza]: 'you see, my daughter, thanks to God you fought, because this is your place [the university]. This is your place'*[116]. (Dandara)

Tereza's outstanding achievement was also her own: "Daughter, you made it! WE made it"[117], she says, and adds: "I'm a BLACK woman, I am poor, my parents struggled a lot [...] now my daughter is a doctor ... [daughter] of a mother who was [Dandara laughs] a nobody"[118].

"Foi um bom jeito de chegar, levando essa mochila especial, cheia de pessoas especiais".

[116] 'Eu fico muito emocionada, né, quando a gente fala assim ... Esse aqui foi ... é! ... o meu grande sonho. Meu grande sonho. Que eu olho assim: o que eu não pude ter, os meus tem, né. Que nem: eu fiquei muito orgulhosa que ela chegou em mim, né, quando foi fazer a *matrícula na USP* ... *ela chegou* em mim e falou assim: "mãe, vâmo comigo fazê a matrícula?" Os pais, né, eu e meu marido. Eu falei assim: "Tereza ... nossa filha ... que presente que cê tá me dando". Nossa [Anna], cê nem imagina como eu fiquei orgulhosa ela assinando a matricula dela lá na USP. Lá que... falei: "você tá vendo, minha filha, graças a deus cê lutou, porque aqui que é seu lugar. Aqui é seu lugar."'

[116] "Filha, você conseguiu! NÓS conseguimos essa vitória."

[118] "Sou uma mulher NEGRA, sou pobre, meus pais teve muita dificuldade [...] hoje minha filha é uma doutora ... de uma mãe [Dandara ri alto] que foi barnabé."

Dandara also reflects about the unfairness in accessing good higher education in Brazil, as the children of the poor have few opportunities to get a place at top universities such as USP like her daughter did:

The university [USP], obviously, is great, right, why not, understand? It's not because one has means, right, only because one has means: why not the poor? [accepted at USP] ... I am from the east part of town, I am poor, my daughter went to a state-funded school, understand ... now she is there, at the big USP, right. How many parents, like, would like their children to be [there] ... but didn't have this opportunity: why they didn't have it?[119] (Dandara)

Dandara is also proud of her daughter's latest accomplishment, giving birth to her first child. About that, she told me:

I am very proud indeed ... it is .... to me ... like ... a [big] fight: I am poor, thanks to God, right, and I am proud, indeed, to live in a poor community such as Vila Dalila which is to me a kind of community, right, more challenging ... but we are winning, thanks to God. My daughter, right, is preparing herself, right and is better each day, right[120]. (Dandara)

Dandara then told me about her own tragic experience of prenatal care and birth, very different to her daughter's experience, and how she suffered when she learned that Tereza was pregnant, concerned that she would have a difficult prenatal and birth experience, as she did.

Tereza "came with suffering"[121], she recalls. During a medical appointment, she was informed by the doctor that her baby was dead when she was three months pregnant. The doctor referred her to a procedure, to

---

[119] "A universidade [USP], lógico, é ótima, né, por que não, entendeu? Não é porque é só os que tem condições [de entrar na USP], né, os que tem condições: por que o pobre não? ... eu sou da zona leste, eu sou pobre, minha filha estudou em escola pública, entendeu ... ela tá lá, tá na grande USP, né. Quantos pais, assim, gostaria que seu filho estivesse ... então não teve essa oportunidade: não teve porque?"
[120] "Eu fico muito orgulhosa sim ... é ... pra mim ... assim ... aquela luta: que eu sou pobre, graças a deus, né, e eu tenho orgulho sim, morando numa comunidade, Vila Dalila, que pra mim é uma comunidade, né, assim, mais difícil ... mas a gente tá vencendo, graças a deus. A minha filha, né, tá se preparando, né, e cada dia melhor, né."
[121] "veio com sofrimento."

be done straight after her consultation, to remove the dead foetus from her womb. Shocked by the news and scared of going through the procedure alone, without telling anyone beforehand, she decided to leave the hospital and speak to her family and husband before going ahead with the procedure.

I didn't ask Dandara about this topic, but she voluntarily sent me a long audio recorded message telling me about her prenatal and birth experience of her first child, Tereza:

> *I had several complications: I was [pregnant for] three months, I didn't know that I was pregnant. My period was normal ... then, when I went to the doctor, at the hospital, the doctor said, right: 'the foetus' – he said it like this – [the foetus] was gone, right. That it was practically ... [the doctor] said that [the foetus] was dead, that I should have it removed, right. And I was so desperate because I was there all alone ... so I said to myself: 'oh, no! I will go home, then I will speak to my mother, right. [I will speak] with my husband, understand? Then I will go to hospital to do the procedure [to remove the material from her womb]. I am alone, I don't know what may happen to me, I am alone. So I will actually go home.' At home, thanks to God, it all happened. As my mother is very experienced, I asked her: 'mother?', as my mother was the mother of twelve children. She said that ... and the doctor said to me: 'you have an infantile uterus. Every time you get pregnant, when you are about three or four months [of pregnancy] you will lose your baby'. And I said to myself: 'God, have mercy', right. Then, you know? [I felt] a real despair, you know? Then I came, I went down to speak with my mother and my mother said to me: 'what did [the doctor] say, my daughter?' When I told my mother that the doctor said that I had an infantile uterus, she told me: 'change doctor. You have to change doctor! If you had an infantile uterus, you wouldn't even be able to get pregnant, right. You wouldn't be pregnant in the first place! You must change doctor!' Thanks to God, I changed: look at my daughter now!*[122] (Dandara)

---

[122] "Eu tive bastante complicação: eu tava de três meses, eu não sabia que eu tava grávida. A minha menstruação descia... aí, quando eu fui ao médico, no hospital, o médico falou, né: "o feto – falou desse jeito – que já tava passando, né. Que já que tava praticamente ... falou que tava morto, que era pra mim fazer a raspagem, né. E eu fiquei tão desesperada que eu tava sozinha ... aí peguei eu falei assim: "ah, não! Eu vou pra minha casa, aí eu converso com a minha mãe, né? Com meu marido, entendeu? Aí [só depois disso] eu vou no hospital, né, faço a raspagem. Eu tô sozinha, eu não sei o que pode acontece comigo, eu tô sozinha! Então eu vou realmente pra casa, né. Aonde, graças a deus, aconteceu. Como a minha mãe é muito

Dandara spent the rest of her pregnancy concerned about her baby. She did not have peace of mind until Tereza was born, a healthy baby. She says: "[During] the pregnancy ... I did bed rest [self-imposed], all those things: one gets tense [about it], right ... and this pregnancy like this [complicated]. Until my baby was born, I couldn't have peace. [...] And [now] my daughter is here!"[123].

Dandara wished she had kept the doctor's referral letter so she could seek justice as she could potentially had an abortion of a healthy baby against her will if she followed the doctor's orders. She told me:

Oh, my colleagues from the factory [where she worked at the time] told me: 'Dandara, sue him!' [the doctor] but I didn't have any proof against him, no proof at all. Because I actually left the piece of paper he gave me for the [miscarriage] cleaning [the referral letter for the procedure] at the door [the reception desk at the hospital]. I was there waiting to be called, for the nurse to call me to do the procedure, can you believe that? I stayed there for a long time, you know, some time, a lot of time until they called me. And then I said to myself: 'you know what, I am leaving here'. I didn't get [a copy of] the paperwork. If only I had the paperwork with me, I could come back there, speak to him [the doctor] ... but you know, you know when you just don't?[124]
(Dandara)

---

vivida eu falei: "mãe?", minha mãe foi mãe de 12 filhos, né. Ela falou assim ... e o médico falou assim: "você tem útero infantil, toda as sua gravidez, quando tiver três, quatro meses, cê vai perdê". Eu eu falei assim: "misericórdia", né? Então, sabe? Aquele desânimo mesmo? Aí eu vim, eu desci, conversei com a minha mãe e a minha mãe falou: "o que que ele falou, minha filha?" Quando eu falei pra minha mãe que o médico falou, que eu tinha útero infantil, ela falou assim: "muda de médico! Pode mudar se médico! Se você tivesse útero infantil, você não ia ficá nem grávida, né. Nem grávida você ia ficá! Pode mudá de médico!" Aonde que, graças a deus, eu mudei: olha minha fia ai!'

[122] "Aí a gravidez ... aí eu fiquei de repouso, aquelas coisa tudo: cê fica com a tensão, né ... e essa gravidez assim ... eu falei assim "meu deus do céu"! Enquanto não nascia, não ficava sossegada. [...] e minha fia tá aí!"

[124] "Ah, meus colegas da fábrica falaram assim: "Dandara, processa!" [processa o médico que encaminhou para a raspagem] mas eu não tive nenhuma prova contra o médico, nenhuma prova. Porque o papel que ele me deu pra retirar, pra fazê uma limpeza, da raspagem, aliás, eu deixei na porta. Eu tava só esperando esse pessoal me chamá, a enfermeira me chamá pra fazê o serviço, acredita numa coisa dessa? Fiquei um tempão, sabe, um tempo menina, fiquei um tempão, pois me chamaram. Aí eu falei: "quer saber de uma coisa, eu vou-me embora". Eu não peguei o papel.

Dandara's birth memories are also traumatic as she had to have a C-section against her will. Her prenatal and birth experiences are not an isolated case. Black women like her are more likely to have inadequate prenatal and birth care and to be more subject to pain compared to white women in Brazil (Leal et al., 2017) and elsewhere such as in the UK, where the death rate for black women from childbirth is five times higher than it is for white women (MBRRACE-UK, 2020, Joint Committee on Human Rights, 2020). According to Pemberton (Anna Freud Centre, 2022) the current statistics around black maternal death in the UK highlights intergenerational links around trauma among black women as black women experience an interruption of their sense of safety during a time when the woman should be joyous and excited. The normalization of black maternal death and violence is a form of intergenerational trauma, she says, because the apprehension of thinking that they will not have a quality service and they are more at risk, experienced by black women around childbirth is passed from one generation of black women to the next. Pemberton also points out that black maternal death is embedded in a health system that discriminates and fails them, and should not be thought as a "black problem"; white people providing medical services to black women in particular should have awareness and accountability of their own bias and internalized racism. Pemberton adds that because of intergenerational trauma, black women's concern about childbirth – including herself as a black woman – exists even before they are pregnant and prior to engaging with health services. That is similar to what Dandara experienced when her daughter became pregnant.

Dandara was concerned that Tereza would endure the same challenges she experienced when her daughter became pregnant. She recalls:

So, I was thinking, my goodness, if Tereza has the same kind of complications that I had ... what if she needs a C-section ... and, in the end, I carried my granddaughter in my arms [Dandara laughs with joy]. It was

---

Se ao menos se eu pegasse o papel, eu poderia vortá lá, conversá com ele ... mas cê sabe quando cê fica assim?"

the most beautiful thing ... This is what is the true beauty, like, of my life[125]. (Dandara)

Fortunately, the daughter's better life conditions gave her the option to have a vaginal birth at home accompanied by skilled professionals. She had a happy and safe experience. Dandara says:

Her birth [her granddaughter, Tereza's daughter] was very beautiful because she [Tereza] didn't want to have her at the hospital, right, because of this pandemic that is going on [the baby was born in 2020]. And we ... me, as the mother, I was highly concerned, right, also because of her age [Tereza's age], you understand? ... They came one midwife and two doulas, right. They came with all the equipment, so I was like – thanks to God – more relaxed[126]. (Dandara)

Dandara's opportunity to witness the joyful birth of her granddaughter helped her to overcome her own traumatic experience of pregnancy and birth. She could not speak about the birth of her granddaughter without comparing Tereza's experience with her own. Her struggles to give a better life to her daughter were worthwhile, as she can see Tereza living very different experiences compared to her own. This brings her happiness and tranquillity at this stage of life. She compares the suffering she felt during her labour with the joy of watching the humanizing birth of her granddaughter:

So I watched my granddaughter's birth – and it was the most beautiful thing, right. She was born at home, understand? (...) Like Tereza said: 'I want to have [the baby] at home'. And I was thinking: heavenly God ... Because I had her, Tereza ... the birth of Tereza ... Tereza came with suffering, like, the baby was overdue, right. And they did an operation on me, right. A C-

---

"Então fiquei pensando: nossa, se a Tereza tiver complicação que nem eu tive ... precisou fazer cesárea (...) e, no fim, eu peguei minha neta! [Dandara gargalha com alegria] Foi a coisa mais linda (...) Isso aí que é a lindeza, assim, da minha vida."
[126] "O nascimento dela [da neta, filha de Tereza] foi muito bonito porque ela [Tereza] não quis ir pro hospital, né, por causa dessa pidemia que tá tendo. E a gente ... eu, como mãe, fiquei muito preocupada, né, pela idade também, entendeu? (...) Vieram uma parteira e duas doula, né. Veio com tudo os aparelho, então eu fiquei mais assim – graças a deus – mais sossegada".

section ... I was expecting to have a natural birth, right. ... My dear, I was suffering, right. They then broke my water, right, and I was not even expecting this thing and then, after all, the baby was overdue. I said: 'Oh, Tereza! You were a fighter before you were born, my daughter!' [Dandara laughs aloud]. Before she was even born, right[127]. (Dandara)

Dandara says, for the second time in our interviews that: "All that I couldn't do, my daughter is now able to do it all"[128]. The better life achieved by both her children makes her proud and fulfilled:

[Her children] they fight, right, they really fight ... and always [having] that support [from their parents that say]: 'study, study and continue!' She [Tereza] keeps on studying, studying, [attending] seminars, right, understand ... there was a book! [the academic book published by Tereza] Look at that: what else should I wish for, right? What else should I wish for?[129] (Dandara)

Dandara treasures her daughter's experiences and even anticipates the joyful ones to come from her granddaughter: "What is nice to say out loud is that Carolina [her granddaughter] will have a beautiful life"[130], she says, as her granddaughter has already had a better start in life compared to herself and Tereza. She insists on telling me how fulfilled her life is now that her

---

[127] "Aí eu vi o nascimento da minha neta – e foi a coisa mais linda, né! Nasceu em casa, entendeu? (...) Que nem ela falou [Tereza]: 'eu quero ter em casa' [o bebê]. E eu pensando: 'meu deus do céu...' Porque eu tive ela, a Tereza ... o nascimento da Tereza .... a Tereza veio com sofrimento, assim, tava passando a hora de nascer, né. E eles fizeram uma cirurgia em mim, né. Cesárea ... eu tava esperando tê normal, né. (...) Minha fia, eu tava em sofrimento, ne. Então estouraram minha bolsa, né, e eu não tava nem esperando isto ai e ai, enfim das conta ela tava passando da hora de nascê. Eu falava: "Eita Tereza! Cê lutou antes de nascer, fia! [Dandara cai no riso]. Foi antes de nascer, né!"
[128] "Tudo o que eu não fiz, minha filha está fazendo."
[129] "[Meus filhos] eles vão pra luta, né, eles vão muito pra luta (...) e sempre aquele apoio mêmo: 'estuda, estuda e continua!' Ela [Tereza] continua estudando, estudando, é palestra aqui, entendeu ... teve livro! Olha que orgulho: o que mais que eu quero, ne? Que mais que eu quero?"
[130] "o que é gostoso de dizer é que a Carolina, vai ter uma história muito bonita."

children have better prospects in life: "I am a woman, indeed. A black woman, right, fulfilled. Ful-filled. With everyone, right, with my family"[131].

When I asked Tereza if she still wished to help her mother in any emotional or material aspect, she told me that she would have liked to help Dandara to pursue her dream of becoming a singer. Tereza said that her mother has a very artistic nature but did not have the chance of doing anything related to it until very recently: "Now she does that [singing] but she started it so late in life … I think that, if she could have started it earlier, she would be more fulfilled"[132]. Tereza also told me that she wished her mother could have a rest now that her children are adults and have their own lives. She would like to help her mother to overcome the emotional weight of caring for all the family members, as her mother is still fighting and worrying for everyone around her.

Rest is very important to mental health especially when someone such as Dandara, a black woman, is at the face of trauma and the violence of everyday racism. As highlighted by Pemberton, being a black person, particularly a black woman like herself, is relentless, draining and upsetting because there is no "quick fix" of racism. Anti-racism work is bigger than oneself, she says, it is legacy work. Therefore, she adds, self-care is highly important. It is important to restore and decompress, to rest as a form of resistance – and enjoy that rest as well – for their own preservation (Anna Freud Centre, 2022).

3.3 Val and Paula

Val told me that she wished her daughter had all the opportunities she did not have. She is conscious of her role in her daughter's successful career and that is empowering to herself. Paula did not share many memories of her childhood, except the one about accompanying her mother to work using public transport, when her mother would struggle to carry her in her arms in crowded buses. Despite not opening herself much, she gave all the credit for her social mobility to her mother. She says her mother taught her to be

---

[131] "Sou uma mulher sim. Uma mulher negra, né, realizada. Re-a-li-za-da. Por todos, né, pela minha família."
[132] "Agora ela faz isso né, mas começou tão tarde … acho que se ela pudesse começar mais cedo talvez ela pudesse ser mais realizada."

the strong woman she is now, to aim for a university degree and to be an independent woman. When I asked if she wished to help her mother in any way, she said that she still wants to be able to purchase a car for Val and told me that her mother can always count on her emotional support.

3.4 Vitória and Helena

Vitória left her first child, Claudia, to be raised by her mother in the northeast when she was one year old. Mother and daughter were never reunited as Vitória lived at her employers' house and struggled to settle in the southeast. Later, she was able to change jobs, work formally and experienced better working conditions and income, but it was too late to have Claudia with her as the mother and daughter relationship was estranged by the long period apart. Vitória did not share with me how she feels about the separation from her daughter. Despite all her efforts providing for Claudia when she was younger, she now lives in poverty, lacking basic needs. Vitória was not able to enjoy life as a grandmother because of the distance between mother and daughter – geographical and emotional.

Vitória struggled to find a job in Campinas after having her second daughter, Helena, but she found one when the baby was about four to five months old – the same job she has been working at since then. Her employers offered her the opportunity to bring the baby to work, gifting her with a cot to put her baby in while she was working in the house. Although mother and child stayed together, Helena resents her mother's absence. She recalls:

> *During my childhood and ALWAYS! [her mother was absent] My mother always worked a lot. She was not very present at home. She worked ... she always left home early in the morning because we always lived very far away from her job ... actually, the place where we lived was very far away from everything, away from the city centre so ... Me, since I was a little girl, to be able to go to school I had to wake up very early in the morning and we ended up coming back home only in the evening because ... all things always followed the commercial opening times so she [her mother] left work and picked me up at school and when we arrived home it was already about 7 pm because the bus services were slow and our house was distant. ... When*

> *I was younger, she [her mother] worked even on Saturdays so we never had much time, like, together at home. [We could be together] only on Sundays, really, but then she had to do things at home: tidy up the house, do the cleaning, organize things and all else. But every time she COULD be present, she was*[133]. (Helena)

Still, daughter and mother have a close relationship and Vitória had a second opportunity to experience motherhood after the separation from her first child. The birth of Helena's first child has been an immense source of joy in Vitória's life lately. After twenty-seven years working for the same family, Vitória has a comfortable life and is able to be more present in Helena's and her grandson's lives. Still, Helena wished she could help Vitória further, if she had the means for that, helping her mother to retire and also, paying for a private medical plan for Vitória:

> *If I could ... I wish she didn't have to work anymore, right, that she didn't have to depend on her salary to live. I would let her have a rest. And, if I could, I would pay for that to happen, and I would also pay for a private medical plan for my mother, as she doesn't have one and every time she needs medical help, it is always a struggle, right, because the health system in Brazil is not the best thing around ... I think that, just by being able to rest [from work] that would be enough to help her emotionally'*[134]. (Helena)

---

[133] "Durante a infância e sempre! [a mãe esteve ausente] A minha mãe sempre trabalhou muito. Ela não era muito presente em casa não. Ela trabalhava ... sempre saiu muito cedo porque a gente sempre morou muito distante do trabalho dela   na verdade, onde a gente morava era muito distante de tudo, era distante do centro então ... Eu também, pra poder ir pra ir pra escola, desde pequenininha, sempre tinha que acordar muito cedo e a gente acabava voltando a noite, porque era ... tudo sempre funcionou no horário comercial então [ela, a mãe] saia do trabalho e ela me pegava na escola e ate chegar em casa era uma 7 horas já porque o ônibus demora e tal, a casa era longe. (...) Quando eu era mais nova ela trabalhava até aos sábados, então a gente nunca teve muito tempo assim juntas em casa. Era mais domingo mesmo e aí ela ainda tinha que fazer as coisas em casa: arrumá a casa, limpá, né, organizar e tudo o mais. Mas ela sempre, quando PÔDE estar, esteve."

[134] "Se eu pudesse (…) eu gostaria que ela não precisasse mais trabalhar, né, que ela não dependesse mais do dinheiro do trabalho pra viver. Eu deixaria ela descansando. E, se eu conseguisse, bancaria tudo e pagaria um convênio médico pra minha mãe, que ela não tem, então sempre que ela precisa tem que ficá passando perrengue, né, porque a saúde do Brasil não é a melhor coisa que existe. (...) eu acho que só dela poder descansar, acho que isso já seria bom pro emocional também."

At the moment Helena cannot help her mother financially – it is the mother who is helping her. When I asked Vitória what else she wished for her daughter that she still has not achieved, she said she wished:

that she had a better salary, right, because her salary is very low for all the things that she does, right. And ... have a better salary, right, that is what we expect, right, a better job because ... she is a teacher and all, but her salary is very low"[135].

She adds that: "people spend four years at university, they get their degree, they spend the money they don't have[136]", reflecting that it is a shame that a person who put so much effort to obtain a degree, like her daughter, will eventually struggle to have a decent salary.

The financial support provided by her mother allows Helena to stay with her baby while she is away from her teaching job, avoiding an early separation of mother and baby if Helena had to find additional sources of income. Vitória has achieved a level of empowerment herself that is helping her to heal her first motherhood experience through her second one. However, the fragility of Helena's trajectory, even after receiving such levels of support, restricts the healing process as Vitória still feels the weight of carrying her daughter towards a better life and Helena feels impotent to help her mother in return, as she has not yet achieved full social mobility.

3.5 Carmem and Julia

The information I gathered from my interviews with Carmem and Julia were very restricted as both women avoided sharing their stories of trauma and their feelings in general. I gathered that the birth of Carmem's grandson has been a great source of joy: "I am very proud of my daughter indeed,

---

[135] "(…) é que ela possa ter um salário melhor, né, porque o salário dela é muito poco pelo tudo que ela faz, né. E... é ter um salário melhor, né, é isso que a gente espera, né, um emprego melhor porque ... ela é professora e tudo, mas o salário é muito poco."

[136] "(...) as pessoas ficam quatro anos numa faculdade, se formando, gastando o que não tem (...)."

especially now that she has given me a grandson"[137], she says. Although she was not able to support her daughter financially, she had an important role supporting her daughter emotionally.

Julia is very grateful for her mother's efforts, and she told me that she received a lot of support and career guidance from Carmem when she decided to pursue a different course at university after one year of her studies. She said her mother is an inspiring force to her and she is very proud that her mother went to university for the first time when she was on her mid-forties. The daughter gave me a glimpse into her mother's eventual source of trauma, but it only went so far: "I had more love, more family support in all the decisions I made … this is something my mother never had"[138], she says.

3.6 Findings

The mothers I interviewed tended to focus their conversations on their daughter's achievements rather than talking about the traumas they have experienced individually or together. Most happy memories are associated with their daughter's educational and professional achievements as well as good experiences of motherhood when daughters became mothers themselves. Many of them postponed or dismissed their own ambitions in favour of their daughters'. They are all very proud of their daughters and rejoiced that they are not trapped in a domestic worker's life like they were, or still are. These women are emotionally fulfilled and empowered by their daughter's success above their own. The mothers that are now grandmothers showed that now, later in life, because their daughters – and sometimes also themselves – have achieved a more comfortable life, they finally have the time and the resources to enjoy their grandchildren. This is particularly important as most mothers were unable to be close to their children when they were young because they had to work long hours. Some even had to separate from their children as having the children living with them was incompatible with the urgency of having full-time jobs that would not give them the time or means to keep their children close to them.

---

[137] "tenho muito orgulho sim e mais ainda agora que ela me deu um netinho lindo."
[138] "eu tive mais carinho, mais apoio familiar em tudo nas minhas decisões … coisa que a minha mãe não teve."

It caught my attention that most of the daughters I interviewed had a good understanding about their mother's lives, sometimes from a time before they were born. Some provided me detailed information such as their mother's age and year group when they stopped going to school, or how old their mothers were when they caught up with their education later in life. Many also had information about their grandmothers, showing a big awareness about their family history and struggles, and good communication between the daughters and the women that preceded them.

Daughters tended to recognize that they had much better opportunities in life compared to their mothers and they were empowered by their mothers in different ways. The daughters have a stronger voice, often speaking for their mothers. Their mother's traumas are imprinted on their lives, and they feel a strong call for justice on behalf of their mothers, sometimes showing a contrast between resentment and companionship, mediated by trauma that guided them to a repairing process that touched both mothers and daughters.

All daughters showed a strong desire to help repairing the emotional scars of their mothers now they have improved their income and social condition. The daughters that experienced more fragile trajectories are more restricted in giving back to their mothers (materially and emotionally), limiting their healing process. Most daughters are already helping their mothers to overcome their traumatic experiences by either providing financial relief or by being a happy presence in their lives – themselves and their children. Mothers and daughters are more present in each other's lives now that some mothers are older and work less, or are retired.

Chapter Four

Knowledge and Love (Conclusion)

Important governmental programmes widened access to higher education in Brazil during the early 2000s, driving many to become the first-generation entrants in university within their families. The role of families in this process is often overlooked. The overall objective of this book was to investigate the role of the families supporting the younger generation to pursue higher education, specifically the role of the mother as a paid domestic worker supporting her daughters, breaking up the cycle of domestic work through higher education. Social mobility among domestic workers is particularly important as paid domestic work is a women's job ghetto, still highly informal and one of the main occupations among vulnerable women in the country; a strong barrier towards empowerment of these women and gender equality. I shifted the gaze from the traditional studies about social mobility between fathers and sons towards women: I interviewed domestic workers and their daughters, the first generation of entrants in higher education within their families, and gathered information about their experiences of social mobility through their life stories.

I showed that the role of the mothers empowering their daughters to pursue higher education was a key element in the process that led to their daughter's social mobility, which otherwise would not have been possible. A variety of forms of support was offered – much beyond income itself, and beyond the reach of government programmes alone – important though the latter might be. The women I interviewed did not benefit from governmental funding programmes or affirmative action policies, and were the first generation to go to university, nonetheless.

My conversations with domestic workers showed me that mothers were more capable of providing support for their children when domestic worker's rights started being protected by law and they were formally employed. When the occupation become more professionalized, mothers were able to work fewer hours, be paid for the overtime worked and have time for themselves and their families. This is notably good for their well-being as they are able to enjoy their grandchildren's presence, a new experience for many of these women, as they were often unable to be present in their children's lives when the children were little because they had to work long hours. Some of the mothers even experienced traumatic separations from their children in their early years. The recently gained "personal space" improved these women's well-being, allowing some of them to look after themselves in different forms, including the pursuit of formal education and even obtaining a higher education degree in the case of one of the women I interviewed.

Although women participants I interviewed have different life stories, when comparing and contrasting them I concluded that they have many similarities, as their lives were shaped by similar contexts. The better life enjoyed by the daughters of domestic workers was possible because their mothers worked long hours, and they coped with difficult working conditions that forced them to be absent from their families. The group of mothers and daughters I interviewed was very special and showed how challenging and specific is the form of social mobility the daughters experienced, breaking the cycle that historically dragged working-class, mostly black women in the country into paid domestic work.

Daughters were driven by their own dreams but also their mother's: these daughters figuratively took their mothers to university with them and lifted them towards happier lives, empowering their mothers too. They started seeing higher education as a real possibility for the first time, no matter their social origin. The *momentum* generated by the democratization of higher education inspired and encouraged not only young but also mature women to pursue formal education. This improved work opportunities in times of job creation and these women's educational accomplishments had a positive impact on their self-esteem. The first-generation university entrants paved the way towards more representativity in the higher education environment, occupying spaces as women and low-income individuals and in one case, also as black women. However, they are still under-represented, especially in public universities, and the fragility of these trajectories – even when receiving such levels of support – has to be highlighted.

I introduced the concept of *intertwined memories* and showed how this mechanism of memory transmission between mothers and daughters led to mutual support between these women, transforming trauma into empowerment. My interviews with mothers and daughters showed that the relationship between them is at the core of repairing trauma. Many of the daughters that were the first-generation entrants in higher education are now mothers themselves, and the transformation achieved through the process of emotional repairing between themselves and their mothers is likely to create a new generation that will share and carry less trauma, very different from the one that has hitherto existed.

I gathered from my conversations with mothers and daughters that are black women, that racial trauma is often overlooked in the early years. It is important that adults interacting with children – at home, at school, in society – help to build a positive sense of self, particularly in racially minoritized children, as they have a strong impact on these children, sometimes for the rest of their lives. Anti-racist practices at the foundation stage and during the early years is an important resource and a form of early intervention at schools, as it has a preventive approach of trauma, aiming to take effect before the trauma is created. Since the global pandemic in 2020, studies have shown that black women in the early years were more affected by inequalities that were deepened. The traumas experienced throughout these challenging years are creating memories that will shape these children's development, future health and happiness, and will potentially extend across generations.

Women who were the first generation of university entrants in Brazil often faced additional pressures which their peers did not from the early days and throughout their lives, and that had an important impact on their well-being. They are making history by occupying spaces at universities that – until very recently – excluded them, but their achievements should not come at a cost to their mental health. The widening access to higher education must come accompanied by transformations within the university and society as a whole, to ensure that all students, regardless of their background, have positive academic and social experiences, supporting long-term and intergenerational change.

To conclude this book, I draw attention to the paradox created by the driving forces behind the social mobility experienced by the daughters of domestic workers. The pursuit of education by the daughters I interviewed was motivated by their determination to have a better life, but equally strong was their will to escape from paid domestic work. As such, they aimed to be the opposite of their mothers, as if distancing themselves from their mothers' life trajectories was a synonym of success. The mothers' sacrifices to support their daughters were driven by the same forces: they did not want their daughters to be what they were themselves. The life trajectory of these mothers led many to downplay their own value, as well as their incredible agency, even as they were key agents in effecting their daughters' process of social mobility.

On a personal level, this journey of intergenerational escape from paid domestic work triggered a series of mutual support initiatives that empowered the mothers and enabled the social mobility of the younger generation. But it also reinforces, unintendedly, the widespread social perception that paid domestic work is a personal failure, not a proper job; that the occupation does not require proper skills as the talents required are inherent in women's/mothers' nature, removing agency from domestic workers as a class and reinforcing gender stereotypes. Ultimately, this perpetuates the perception that paid domestic work is not equal to other working-class occupations, and draws attention away from improving the conditions of those in the profession, ultimately contributing to its devaluation. Broader gains are thus contingent on this escape from paid domestic work being accompanied by renewed demands for improved, dignified working conditions for the occupation, which continues to be characterized by high levels of informality and exploitation. For that, domestic workers and their daughters as well as society as a whole have an important role promoting further change, which is currently more urgent than ever as the country's struggling economy, aggravated by the pandemic and compounded by a conservative government, jeopardizes the hard-fought progress towards these women's empowerment and social mobility.

REFERENCES

Acciari, L. (2018). Paradoxes of Subaltern Politics: Brazilian Domestic Workers' Mobilisations to Become Workers and Decolonise Labour. A thesis submitted to the Department of Gender Studies of the London School of Economics for the degree of Doctor of Philosophy, London, July 2018. http://etheses.lse.ac.uk/3839/1/Acciari__paradoxes-of-subaltern politics.pdf [accessed 21/02/2023]

Adão, C. R. (2018). *Territórios de morte – Homicídio, raça e vulnerabilidade social*. São Paulo: Novas Edições Acadêmicas.

Alcoba, N. (2021). Argentina's New Pensions Programme Pays Women for Caregiving. *AlJazeera*, 5 August. Available at: https://www.aljazeera.com/economy/2021/8/5/argentinas-new-pensions-programme-pays-women-for-caregiving [accessed 21/02/2023]

Almeida, S. (2019). *Racismo Estrutural*. Feminismos Plurais series, D. Ribeiro (Ed.). São Paulo: Pólen Livros.

Alves Cordeiro, A. L. (2013). Ações afirmativas na educação superior: mulheres negras cotistas e mobilidade social. *Revista Pedagógica Unochapecó*, 15(30), 297–314.

Amparo Alves, J. (2018). *The Anti-Black City*. Minneapolis (MN): University of Minnesota Press.

Anna Freud Centre (2022). Early Years in Mind: Trauma and Repair Webinar. 16 June 2022. With Liz Pemberton, Abi Miranda, Sarah Peter, Dina Koschorreck. Available at: https://youtu.be/fNQcMebZYto [accessed 21/02/2023]

References

Bar-Haim, S. (2021). *The Maternalists – Psychoanalysis, Motherhood, and the British Welfare State*. Philadelphia (PA): University of Pennsylvania Press.

Batista, J. R. M., Leite, E. L., Torres, A. R. R. and Camino, L. (2014). Black and Northeasterners: Similarities in Racial and Regional Stereotypes (in Portuguese). *Psicologia Política*, 14(30), 325–345. Available at: http://pepsic.bvsalud.org/pdf/rpp/v14n30/ v14n30a08.pdf [accessed 21/02/2023]

Berth, J. (2019). *Empoderamento*. Feminismos Plurais series, D. Ribeiro (Ed.). São Paulo: Pólen Livros.

Billingham, S. (2018) (Ed.). *Access to Success and Social Mobility through Higher Education – A Curate's Egg?* Bingley, UK: Emerald Publishing.

Bizerril, M. (2018). A interiorização das Universidades Federais foi um acerto estratégico para o Brasil. *Notícias UNB*, 24 October. Available at: https://noticias.unb.br/artigos-main/2580-a-interiorizacao-das-universidades-federais-foi-um-acerto-estrategico-para-o-brasil [accessed 21/02/2023]

Brito, D. (2018). Cotas foram revolução silenciosa no Brazil, afirma especialista. Agência Brasil, 27 May. Available at: https://agenciabrasil.ebc.com.br/educacao/noticia/2018-05/cotas-foram-revolucao-silenciosa-no-brasil-afirma-especialista [accessed 21/02/2023]

Canuto, O. and Zhang, P. (2021). Global Recovery May Not be Enough for Latin America. Center for Macroeconomics & Development, 5 June. Available at: https://www.cmacrodev.com/global-recovery-may-not-be-enough-for-latin-america/ [accessed 21/02/2023]

Carvalho, C. H. A. (2013). A mercantilização da educação superior Brasileira e as estratégias de mercado das instituições lucrativas. *Revista brasileira de educação*, 18(54), 761–801.

Collins, P. H. (2000). The Power of Self-definition. In P. H. Collins (Ed.) *Black Feminist Thought* (pp. 97–121). New York (NY): Routledge.

Cosme, I. (2021). Em mudança histórica, maioria dos novos alunos da USP é de escolas públicas. Estado de S.Paulo. 4 June. Available at: https://educacao.estadao.com.br/noticias/geral,pela-primeira-vez-na-historia-maioria-dos-novos-alunos-da-usp-e-de-escolas-publicas,70003736785 [accessed 21/02/2023]

Da Silva, C. (2018). Feminismo Negro – de onde viemos: aproximações de uma memória. In: H. B. D Hollanda (Ed.), *Explosão feminista – arte, cultura, política e universidade* (2nd ed., pp. 252–260). São Paulo: Companhia das Letras.

Duffy, M. (2007). Doing the Dirty Work: Gender, Race, and Reproductive Labor in Historical Perspective. *Gender & Society*, 21(3), 313–336. doi: 10.1177/0891243207300764.

European Commission (2015). Pension Adequacy Report: current and future income adequacy in old age in the EU. Volume I. Available at: https://ec.europa.eu/social/BlobServlet?docId=14529&langId=en [accessed 23/03/2023]

Fish, J. N. (2017). *Domestic Workers of the World Unite! A Global Movement for Dignity and Human Rights*. New York (NY): New York University Press.

Fonseca, R. M. (2018). Democracia e acesso à universidade no Brasil: um balanço da história recente (1995–2017). *Educar em Revista*, 34(71), 299–307. https://doi.org/10.1590/0104-4060.62654 [accessed 21/02/2023]

Gates Foundation (2017). *Women's Economic Empowerment: Brazil.* Available at: https://www.gatesfoundation.org/equal-is-greater/case-study/brazil/ [accessed 21/02/2023]

Geledés (2021). A Educação de Meninas Negras em Tempo de Pandemia: o Aprofundamento das Desigualdades. Available at: https://www.geledes.org.br/a-educacao-de-meninas-negras-em-tempos-de-pandemia-o-aprofundamento-das-desigualdades-o-livro/ [accessed 21/02/2023]

Ginn, J. (2001). Risk of Social Exclusion in Later Life: How Well do the Pension Systems of Britain and the US Accommodate Women's Paid and Unpaid Work? *International Journal of Sociology and Social Policy*, 21(4–6), pp. 212–244. https://doi.org/10.1108/01443330110789501 [accessed 21/02/2023]

Goldstein, J., Freud, A. and Solnit, A. J. (1980a). *Before the Best Interests of the Child.* London: Burnett Books.

Goldstein, J., Freud, A. and Solnit, A. J. (1980b). *Beyond the Best Interests of the Child.* London: Burnett Books.

Goldthorpe, J., Llewellyn, C. and Payne, C. (1987). *Social Mobility and Class Structure in Modern Britain.* Oxford: Clarendon Press.

Gopinath, G. (2021). Managing Divergent Recoveries. IMF Blog, 6 April. Available at: https://blogs.imf.org/2021/04/06/managing-divergent-recoveries/ [accessed 21/02/2023]

Grigera, J. (2017). Populism in Latin America: Old and New Populisms in Argentina and Brazil. *International Political Science Review*, 38(4), 441–455.

Hengeveld, M. (2015). Nike's Girl Effect: The Myth of the Economically Empowered Adolescent Girl. *Aljazeera America*, July 20. Available at:

http://america.aljazeera.com/opinions/2015/7/nikes-girl-effect.html [accessed 21/02/2023]

Hines, B. (2000). *A Kestrel for a Knave*. London: Penguin.

Hirsch, M. (2012). *The Generation of Postmemory – Writing and Visual Culture After the Holocaust*. New York (NY): Columbia University Press.

IBGE – Instituto Brasileiro de Geografia e Estatística (2018). Estatísticas de Gênero – Indicadores Sociais das Mulheres no Brasil. Estudos e Pesquisas – Informação Demográfica e Socioeconômica n.38. https://biblioteca.ibge.gov.br/visualizacao/livros/liv101551_informativo.pdf [accessed 21/02/2023]

IBGE – Instituto Brasileiro de Geografia e Estatística (2019). Desigualdades Sociais por Cor ou Raça no Brasil. Estudos e Pesquisas – Informação Demográfica e Socioeconômica n.41. Available at: https://biblioteca.ibge.gov.br/visualizacao/livros/liv101681_informativo.pdf [accessed 21/02/2023]

ILO – International Labour Organization (2018). Domestic Work: Convention No 189 on Domestic Workers Ratified by Brazil, 1 February. Available at: https://www.ilo.org/global/about-the-ilo/newsroom/news/WCMS_616549/lang--en/index.htm [accessed 21/02/2023]

IPEA – Instituto de Pesquisa Econômica Aplicada (2017). Retrato das Desigualdades de Gênero e Raça: 1995–2015. Available at: https://www.ipea.gov.br/portal/images/stories/PDFs/170306_retrato_das_desigualdades_de_genero_raca.pdf [accessed 21/02/2023]

IPEA – Instituto de Pesquisa Econômica Aplicada (2019). Os Desafios do Passado no Trabalho Doméstico do Século XXI: Reflexões para o caso brasileiro a partir dos dados da PNAD contínua. Available at: https://repositorio.ipea.gov.br/bitstream/11058/9538/1/td_2528.pdf [accessed 21/02/2023]

Jensen, G. (2010). *Política de cotas raciais em universidades brasileiras – entre a legitimidade e a eficácia.* Curitiba: Juruá.

Joint Committee on Human Rights, 2020. Black people, racism and human rights. Available at: https://committees.parliament.uk/publications/ 3376/ documents/32359/default/ [accessed 21/02/2023]

Labaree, D. F. (1997). Public Goods, Private Goods: The American Struggle Over Educational Goals. *American Educational Research Journal*, 34(1), 39–81. Available at: https://web.stanford.edu/~dlabaree/publications/Public_Goods_Private _Goods.pdf [accessed 21/02/2023]

Leal, M. D. C., da Gama, S. G. N., Pereira, A. P. E., Pacheco, V. E., do Carmo, C. N. and Santos, R. V. (2017). A cor da dor: iniquidades raciais na atenção pré-natal e ao parto no Brasil, *Cad. Saúde Pública* vol. 33 suppl. 1 Rio de Janeiro 2017 Epub 24 July 2017 https://doi.org/10.1590/0102-311x00078816 [accessed 21/02/2023]

Lima, M. and Prates, I. (2019). Emprego doméstico e mudança social: reprodução e heterogeneidade na base da estrutura ocupacional brasileira. *Tempo social: revista de sociologia da USP*, 31(2), 149–171.

Lorde, A. (1984). *Sister Outsider: Essays and Speeches.* Trumansburg (NY): Crossing Press.

Machado Chaves, F. (2000). Outros Olhares em Escolas Públicas: As Relações Sociais de Trabalho sob a Ótica de Merendeiras e Serventes. *Trabalho & Educação*, Vol. 7. Belo Horizonte. Jul/Dez 2000. Available at: https://periodicos.ufmg.br/index.php/trabedu/article/view/9208/6628 [accessed 21/02/2023]

Magalhães, V. B. (2015). Nordestinos na Zona Leste de São Paulo: subjetividade e redes de migrantes. TRAVESSIA – Revista do Migrante No 76, January–June. Available at:

https://www.researchgate.net/publication/329252144_MAGALHAES_Valeria_B_Nordestinos_na_Zona_Leste_de_Sao_Paulo_subjetividade_e redes de migrantes_Travessia_Publicacao_CEM_ano_XXVIII_n_76_jan-jun2015 [accessed 21/02/2023]

Marques, R. M., Ximenez, S. B. and Ugino, C. K. (2018). Lula and Dilma Governments in Terms of Social Security and Access to Higher Education. *Brazilian Journal of Political Economy*, 38(3), 526–547. https://dx.doi.org/10.1590/0101-35172018-2784 [accessed 21/02/2023]

Mbembe, A. (2003). Necropolitics. *Public Culture*, 15(1), 11–40.

MBRRACE-UK (2020). Saving Lives, Improving Mothers' Care 2020: Lay Summary. Available at: https://www.npeu.ox.ac.uk/assets/downloads/mbrrace-uk/reports/maternal-report-2020/MBRRACE-UK_Maternal_Report_Dec_2020_v10_ONLINE_VERSION_1404.pdf [accessed 21/02/2023]

McKnight, A. (2015). *Downward Mobility, Opportunity Hoarding and the 'Glass Floor'*. Research report. Social Mobility and Child Poverty Commission. Available at: https://dera.ioe.ac.uk/23370/1/Downward_mobility_opportunity_hoarding_and_the_glass_floor.pdf [accessed 21/02/2023]

Melleiro, W. and Heuser, C. (2020). *Care for Those who Take Care of You: Domestic Workers in Brazil*. FES Connect. https://www.fes-connect.org/people/brazil-domestic-workers [accessed 21/02/2023]

Moreira Damasceno, A. and de Andrade, A. M. (2016). Análise do Sistema de Cotas raciais no Brasil como Ações Afirmativas Aliadas ao Direito Geral de Igualdade. *Revista Brasileira de Direitos e Garantias Fundamentais*, 2(1), 1–18.

Moeller, K. (2018). *The Gender Effect – Capitalism, Feminism, and the Corporate Politics of Development*. Oakland (CA): University of California Press

Pastore, J. (1982). *Inequality and Social Mobility in Brazil*. Madison (WI): University of Wisconsin Press.

Pastore, J. and Valle Silva, N. (2000). *Mobilidade social no Brasil*. São Paulo: Makron.

Picanço, F. (2016). Juventude e Acesso ao Ensino Superior no Brasil – Onde está o alvo das políticas de ação afirmativa. *Latin American Research Review*, 51(1), 109–131, 294–295, 299. Available at: https://muse.jhu.edu/article/617803 [accessed 21/02/2023]

Pollak, M. (1993). *Une Identité blesse – Etudes de sociologie et d'histoire*. Paris: Métailié.

Rara, P. (2019). Eu, empregada doméstica: a senzala moderna é o quartinho da empregada. Belo Horizonte: Letramento.

Ribeiro, D. (2018). *Quem tem medo do feminismo negro?* (4th ed.) São Paulo: Companhia das Letras.

Russell, B. (2009). *On Education*. London: Routledge.

Sarlo, B. (2005). Tiempo passado. Buenos Aires: Siglo XXI.

Silva, M. A. de M., Melo, B. M. de M. and De Moraes, L. A. (2016). Saindo das sombras – mulheres sitiantes paulistas. Política & Sociedade, suppl. Edicao Especial; Florianopolis Vol. 15, (2016): 179–207. DOI:10.5007/2175-7984.2016v15nesp1p179

Skeggs, B. (2002). *Formations of Class and Gender – Becoming Respectable*. Thousand Oaks (CA): Sage.

Sriprakash, A., Rudolph S. and Gerrard J. (2022). *Learning Whiteness: Education and the Settler Colonial State.* London: Pluto Press.

Stephens, R. C. (2021). *Educational Leadership and the Global Majority: Decolonising Narratives.* London: Palgrave MacMillan.

Stuart, M. (2012). *Social Mobility and Higher Education: The Life Experiences of First Generation Entrants in Higher Education.* Stoke-on-Trent, UK: Trentham Books.

United Nations (2015). Universal Declaration of Human Rights. Available at: https://www.un.org/en/udhrbook/pdf/udhr_booklet_en_web.pdf [accessed 21/02/2023]

United Nations (2014). The State of Food Insecurity in the World. Available at: https://www.fao.org/3/i4030e/i4030e.pdf [accessed 21/02/2023]

United Nations (2020). Policy Brief: The Impact of COVID-19 on Women. 9 April. Available at:
https://www.unwomen.org/en/digital-library/publications/2020/04/policy-brief-the-impact-of-covid-19-on-women
[accessed 21/02/2023]

Wise, J. B. (2007). Introduction: Empowerment as a Response to Trauma. In: M. Bussey and J. B. Wise (Eds.), *Trauma Transformed: An Empowerment Response* (pp. 1–12) New York (NY): Columbia University Press.

Xavier, C. F. (2019). História e historiografia da Educação de Jovens e Adultos no Brasil - inteligibilidades, apagamentos, necessidades, possibilidades. Revista Brasileira De História Da Educação, 19, e068. Available at:
https://www.scielo.br/j/rbhe/a/mZx7pP7TQFrm7vf63TJgkmr/abstract/?lang=pt [accessed 21/02/2023]